GENISES THROUGH DEUTERONOMY

CHOSEN

Also by Jack J. Blanco:

The Clear Word
The Clear Word for Kids
The Clear Word—Psalms and Proverbs
The Clear Word—The Gospel of John
The Easy English Clear Word
Savior. Four Gospels. One Story.
Visions and Dreams
Witness

Harmony and Chronology of the Old Testament:

Book 1: *Chosen*
Book 2: *Warriors*
Book 3: *Kings*
Book 4: *Survivors*

To order, call **1-800-765-6955.**
Visit us at **www.AutumnHousePublishing.com** for information on
other Autumn House® products.

GENESIS THROUGH DEUTERONOMY

CHOSEN

Harmony and Chronology of the Old Testament, Book 1

JACK J. BLANCO

Autumn
House® Publishing
www.autumnhousepublishing.com
A Division of **REVIEW AND HERALD® PUBLISHING**
Since 1861

This book was
Edited by Gerald Wheeler
Copyedited by Delma Miller
Cover Design by Derek Knecht/Review and Herald® Design Center
Cover Illustration by Harry Anderson
Interior Design by Derek Knecht/Review and Herald® Design Center
Typeset: Bembo 11/13

PRINTED IN U.S.A.

17 16 15 14 13   5 4 3 2 1

Library of Congress Cataloging-in-Publication Data
Blanco, Jack J., 1929-
   Chosen : harmony and chronology of the Old Testament / Jack J. Blanco.
      pages cm
   Includes bibliographical references and index.
   ISBN 978-0-8127-0510-2 (alk. paper)
   1. Bible stories, English--Old Testament. 2. Bible. Old Testament--Chronology. I. Title.
   BS550.3.B57 2013
   221.6'5--dc23
                              2013014916

ISBN 978-0-8127-0510-2

Dedication

*This small volume is dedicated to
Jesus, my Savior and Friend,*

*and to my wife, Marion June,
whose encouragement, kindness, and love
will never be forgotten.*

Acknowledgments

I wish to express my sincere thank-you to:
Jolena King, for reading the manuscript and for her valuable suggestions.
Star Steven, for her editorial skill in preparing the manuscript for publication.
Gerald Wheeler, Review and Herald editor, and
Jeannette Johnson, for her timely communications from the publishing house.

Contents

Preface

Using a format similar to *Savior* (covering the four Gospels) and *Witness* (the remainder of the New Testament), Jack J. Blanco has written a harmony and chronology of the Old Testament as the last set of his trilogy of the Bible for young adults who like to read narratives.

This is the first of four volumes that include:

Books 1 and 2: the Patriarchs section, which begins with Adam and ends with David, and

Books 3 and 4: the Kings section, which starts with Solomon and concludes with Malachi.

Together with the New Testament volumes, the *Harmony and Chronology of the Old Testament* books complete Blanco's Narrative Bible in Chronological Sequence series.

Introduction

Narratives are important to postmodern adult readers. For this purpose, I have shortened repetitive and redundant details in the scriptural narrative without loss of content. Where commentators differ over some noncrucial expression of the central theme of a passage, I have paraphrased the narrative in ways to make the biblical story applicable for current readers.

In addition, I have harmonized the overlapping events in Samuel, Kings, and Chronicles into one story. At times it was necessary to transpose a verse or two within a short passage to make the passage read more smoothly and for better understanding.

While the book of Samuel delineates the sequence of events leading the 12 tribes of Israel into a nation with a king, the primary focus of Kings is on government and rulers. And while Chronicles also deals with kings, its main focus is on the nation's spirituality and its relationship to God. In some cases the history of each king is so brief that the overall narrative becomes fragmented. In order to avoid this, especially with the quick succession of the last kings of Israel and Judah, I have provided a more reader-friendly historical account. And where there is a question about which Assyrian king actually took Samaria, I felt it best simply to say "the king of Assyria."

Although I could have inserted many prophetic messages from Isaiah, Jeremiah, and other prophetic books into the chronological narrative of the final years of Israel and Judah in the harmonized chronology of Kings and Chronicles, it would have fragmented the prophetic books themselves. Therefore, I have left such books as Isaiah and Jeremiah intact and placed them as entire units in the general chronological sequence.

Psalms, Proverbs, and Song of Solomon appear after Kings and Chronicles to stay with the general flow of history. For instance, to place every part of the book of Psalms in its precise sequence would require dividing them into segments, destroying their familiarity as a whole. Furthermore, I have reduced the redundancy in the Psalms, with their lengthy references to war or the threat of attack, so as to enable the reader to grasp the central thrust of the writer.

When it comes to the prophets, Isaiah's ministry spanned approximately 60 years, during which time other prophets appeared, creating some overlapping of messages. To insert the writings of the other prophets into the book of Isaiah would needlessly confuse the reader. The same applies to the books of Ezekiel and Jeremiah, which need to be kept intact, since that is what the reader is familiar with.

While it is not possible to present a precise chronological sequence of each Bible passage without dissecting some of the books as mentioned above, I have maintained the overall flow of events to create a reliable narrative.

To the glory of God,

Jack J. Blanco

one

Creation

In six consecutive 24-hour days God beautified our planet. He flooded it with light, gave it an atmosphere, gathered the waters into oceans, and covered it with grass and trees. In addition He put the sun, moon, and stars in the sky and created birds, fish, animals, and, finally, human beings, both male and female. God began by molding a man out of clay and forming him in His own image. Then He breathed life into the clay, and the man became a living being. God named the man Adam and put him in charge of everything on earth.

After God had made a beautiful garden called Eden for Adam to live in, He told the man that he could eat from all the fruit trees except the one in the middle of the garden. The Lord brought the birds and animals to Adam and asked him to name them. As Adam did so, he noticed that all the animals were in pairs, and he began to feel lonely.

Then God said, "Adam, too, wants a companion and needs one." So God put the man to sleep, opened his side, took out a rib, and from it shaped a woman. Then God woke Adam up and introduced the two, and Adam was extremely happy to have such a beautiful companion and friend.

Adam looked at his companion and said, "God made you from one of my ribs, which makes you part of my body." (Later he would name her Eve.) This happened on the sixth day of the week. On the seventh day, God looked at everything He had made and was pleased, so He rested from His work, blessed the seventh day, and made it holy. That is how the weekly cycle began (Gen. 1:1-2:25; see also John 1:1-3; Eph. 3:9; Col. 1:16; Ps. 33:9; Heb. 11:3).

The Beginning of Sin

One day Eve stopped and admired the forbidden tree in the middle of the garden, and as she did, Satan spoke to her through a beautifully colored winged snake resting in the tree. "Hello, Eve," he said. "Didn't God tell you not to eat the fruit of this tree?"

Surprised that the snake could talk, Eve replied without hesitation, "God said that we could eat from all of the trees except this one and that we shouldn't even touch it. If we eat from this tree, we will die."

"God lied to you," Satan said. "He knows that if you eat from this tree, you'll understand as much as He does. Look at what eating from this tree did for me!"

Eve didn't realize she was being deceived, but she couldn't deny what she was seeing, so she ate the fruit. Then she took some to her husband, and even though he knew that what she had done was wrong and that she would die, he decided to die with her. Accepting the fruit, he ate it.

That evening they heard God walking in the garden, coming to see them, so they hid among the trees. "Adam, where are you?" God called to them. "Why are you and Eve hiding from Me?"

"We're naked, so we're afraid to come out to see You," Adam tried to explain.

"Adam, did you eat from the tree I told you not to?"

"Eve is to blame," Adam replied. "She's the one who brought the fruit to me and urged me to eat it. So I did."

God turned to Eve and asked, "Why did you do this?"

"The snake You created tricked me into it."

Then God said to the snake, "Because Satan used you to deceive Eve, you have become a symbol of evil and will lose your wings and no longer be as beautiful as you are now. You will slither on the ground and be feared by animals and people. I will not only make Eve's offspring afraid of you but will put in their hearts a hatred of what you represent." Then, referring to Satan's activity, God said to the snake, "You will strike at the heel of one of her descendants, but He will crush your head."

Turning back to the woman, God continued, "It will be painful for you to have children, but in spite of this, you will long for a husband and a family."

To Adam God announced, "Because you listened to your wife instead of to Me, your life will be one of toil, and when it's over, you will return to dust."

Then God fashioned sheepskins for Adam and Eve to cover their nakedness, and He sent them out of the garden. He stationed angels with flaming swords at the entrance to keep the couple away from the tree of life so that they couldn't eat from it and become immortal sinners (Gen. 3; see also 1 Tim. 2:13, 14; Rom. 5:12).

Murder

Adam and Eve's first son was Cain, who loved to work the fields. Their second son was Abel, who cared for the sheep. As week by week they worshipped the Lord the time of year came for a special offering. Cain brought what he had grown in the fields, and Abel followed God's instructions and brought a lamb.

Abel's offering pleased God, because the young man had obeyed the Lord. But the Lord was not happy with Cain's offering, because Cain had brought what he thought was best. When Cain became upset at God's response, the Lord asked him, "Why are you angry? If you had done what I asked you to do, your offering would have been accepted, but you decided to do it your own way. Sin is always at the door, waiting to come in and be your master, so you need to keep the door closed."

One day Cain asked Abel to take a walk with him in the field, and when Abel did, Cain attacked and killed him. The Lord saw what had happened, so the next day He asked Cain, "Where is your brother?"

"How should I know? I'm not my brother's keeper!"

"Why did you kill him?" the Lord continued. "His blood is calling out for justice. From now on the soil will not produce for you as easily as it did before, because of what you have done, and wherever you go, you will not be welcome."

"This punishment isn't fair," Cain protested. "It's all out of proportion to what I did. You've turned against me. Now others will feel free to kill me."

The Lord still loved Cain, so He put a mark on him and said, "Anyone who kills Cain will be punished seven times more than he was."

Then Cain left the area near Eden and, with his wife, headed east, where he settled. He decided to build a city, and while he was constructing it, he had a son whom he named Enoch, and he also called the city "Enoch" after his son.

Several generations later Lamech, a descendant of Cain, was born. When he grew up, he took two wives, and one day when he came home, he said to them, "I've just killed one young man for hitting me and another one for insulting me." Then he added arrogantly, "If the Lord will punish anyone who kills Cain seven times more than He punished Cain for killing his brother, He will punish anyone who kills me 77 times more."

When Adam and Eve had a child whom they named Seth, they said, "God has given us another son to take the place of Abel." Seth obeyed the Lord, and when he grew up, he had sons and daughters who followed his example. They felt their need of God and drew very close to Him (Gen. 4).

Adam's Descendants

God had created Adam in His image and likeness, but when Adam had children, they were born in *his* image and likeness, with a tendency to sin. Adam was 130 years old when Seth was born; he lived another 800 years. He had many sons and daughters and died when he was 930 years old.

Seth lived 912 years, and each patriarch after him a long life. The longest-lived patriarch was Methuselah, who lived 969 years. His father was Enoch, who had walked so close to God that when he was only 365 years old the Lord took him to heaven.

Methuselah's grandson was Noah. He was 500 years old when his son Japheth was born, followed by two other sons, Shem and Ham (Gen. 5).

Wickedness Increases

As the population increased, men took as many wives as they chose. When those who loved the Lord saw how beautiful the unbelieving women were, they also married as many as they wanted.

Hurt by what He saw, the Lord said, "My Spirit will not work endlessly with these people. I will give them another 120 years to see what they will do."

When the Lord saw that the people were becoming more and more wicked and that their thoughts were evil all the time, He was really saddened. It pained Him to see that the descendants of Adam, whom He had created in His own image, had degenerated so much and had become so violent and wicked. Sin had affected everything that God had made—even the animals had changed.

God said to Himself, "My Spirit can't get through to these people anymore. I will have to put an end to the violence and wickedness on this planet by destroying what I made, everything from humans to animals."

But a few still pleased God, including Noah and his family (Gen. 6:1-8).

Noah

Noah was a good man who lived close to God during this time of wickedness. He had three sons, each of whom was married.

God told Noah what He was planning to do. "I see all the evil that's going on," He said. "I need to put an end to this immorality, killing, and violence by bringing a worldwide flood on the earth. So I want you to build a boat for yourself and your family. Make it out of cypress wood and cover it with tar, inside and out. It should be 450 feet long, 75 feet wide, and 45 feet high, with compartments on the lower, middle, and upper levels. Leave an 18-inch space between the roof and the sides for light and air, and put a door in the side. The flood will cover the whole earth and destroy every living thing.

"I will watch over you and your family. Take them into the boat, and also bring pairs of all the animals and birds that I will send to you. Stock the boat with food for yourselves and them."

So that's what Noah did (Gen. 6:9-22).

The Flood

He was 600 years old when he finished building the large boat, and God said to him, "Take your family into the boat, and let the animals come in that I am sending you."

Noah did what God told him to do. For one week nothing happened, and the people outside the boat laughed because Noah was now locked in and couldn't get out because God had closed the door. Then it began to rain, and it rained for 40 days and nights, flooding the whole planet—even the mountains were under water. The only ones left alive were Noah and his family and the animals inside the boat. For 150 days the flood covered the earth before the water began to recede (Gen. 7).

After the rain stopped, a wind helped to dry up the water, and the tops of mountains appeared. Noah's boat came to rest on one of the mountains of Ararat, but he waited another 40 days before checking to see if the valleys were dry. Then he sent out a raven, but it came back, because it could find no place to land. A week later he sent out a dove, and it also returned. After another week he let the dove out again. This time it brought back a little leaf in its mouth. When Noah released the dove after one more week, it stayed away. So Noah looked outside again and saw that the valley was dry.

God had watched over Noah and his family, and now that the floodwaters were gone, He said to Noah, "It's time for you and your family to leave the boat and let the animals go." The first thing Noah did outside the boat was to build an altar, sacrifice some animals, and worship God, thanking Him for saving them. Pleased, God said, "Never again will I destroy the earth with a flood, no matter how bad things become! As long as the planet remains, there will be seedtime and harvest, winter and summer, day and night" (Gen. 8).

The Rainbow

God blessed Noah and said, "Enlarge your family and don't worry about the animals, because I have told them not to harm you. Your descendants should not hurt each other, and there should be no bloodshed, but if a person murders another, they should be killed. You are allowed to kill animals but only for food, and don't eat the meat that still has blood in it.

"As a sign of My promise not to destroy the earth again by a flood, I will put a rainbow in the sky. It will remind you that there will never be a global flood like this again" (Gen. 9:1-17).

Noah's Descendants

Noah and his three sons and their descendants eventually repopulated the whole world. They farmed and planted vineyards. One day Noah drank some grape juice that had fermented, and he got drunk. He took off his clothes and lay down naked in the middle of the tent. His son Ham came in and saw his father, then told his two brothers about it. They went to the tent and walked in backward, holding a sheet behind them, and dropped it on their father to cover his nakedness. When Noah woke up and learned what had happened, he blessed Shem and Japheth, but could not bless Ham because of what he had done.

Noah was 600 years old when the Flood came, and he lived another 350 years and died when he was 950 years old (Gen. 9:18-29).

Japheth was the father of the Gentiles, who scattered through many lands. Ham was the father of the Canaanites, with such powerful leaders as Nimrod, who built the cities of Babel and Nineveh and whose territory included the cities of Sodom and Gomorrah. Shem was the father of the ancestors of Abraham, from whom came Jesus Christ (Gen. 10; 11:10-25; see also Luke 3:23-38).

A City

At that time everyone spoke the same language. Some went east and settled in the plains of Babylon and said, "Let's make a name for ourselves by constructing a city with towers so high and strong that no flood can ever destroy them." So they began building. Then God came down to see what was going on and said, "If they succeed at this, they will think they can do anything. Let's give them different languages so they can't understand one another." That's what God did, and when the people couldn't communicate with one another, they had to stop building. That's why the city is called Babel (meaning "confusion"), because that's where the different languages began.

Then they grouped themselves according to their new languages and from there traveled to different parts of the earth (Gen. 11:1-9).

two

Abraham

Terah lived in the city of Ur, southeast of Babylon, and had three sons, Abram, Nahor, and Haran. One day God told Abram to leave Ur and move to the land of Canaan, and when Abram told his father what God had said, Terah decided to take the whole family and go with him. So Abram, with his wife, Sarai (who was also his half sister), Nahor and his family, and the children of Haran (who had previously died) left Ur with their servants, flocks, and herds and made their way as far as the city of Haran. They decided to stay there for a while, and it was here that Abram's father, Terah, died at 205 years old (Gen. 11:26-32).

Then the Lord repeated what He had told Abram before: "Leave this country and go to the land I will show you. I will make a great nation from your descendants, bless those who bless you, and set Myself against those who are against you. Through one of your descendants, all families of the earth will be blessed."

Abram was 75 years old when he and Sarai departed Haran, but the rest of the family decided to stay there, except his nephew, Lot, who went with him. From Haran, Abram traveled southwest toward the land of Canaan to Shechem, where the giant terebinth oaks of Moreh stood. The Lord appeared to him and said, "This is the land I will give you." So Abram built an altar there and worshipped the Lord. Then he headed south to Bethel and built another altar, and from Bethel he continued to move south (Gen. 12:1-9).

Famine

About this time a famine struck the land. To get away from it and preserve his flocks and herds, Abram crossed the border into Egypt. Once there he said to Sarai, "You're a very beautiful woman, and I'm afraid that someone will kill me to get you. So tell people that you're my sister (instead of my half sister). That way you'll save my life."

It happened just as Abram suspected. When the Egyptians saw how beautiful Sarai was, they took her to Pharaoh, and because of her, they treated Abram, his servants, and his animals well. But the Lord brought sickness on Pharaoh and his family, and God told Pharaoh in a dream that Sarai was Abram's wife, not his sister. In the morning Pharaoh called for Abram and demanded, "Why didn't you tell me she was your wife? I might have made her one of my wives. So take her and be on your way!" (Gen. 12:10-20).

Abram and Lot

Then Abram left Egypt and returned to Canaan, traveling north to Bethel, where he had built an altar to the Lord. His nephew, Lot, who had been with him all this time, also had servants and large herds and flocks. One day their servants began to fight over grazing rights. Abram said to Lot, "There's no need for this—there's room enough for all our herds and flocks. You pick the part of the country you want, and I'll go in the opposite direction." Lot decided to take the section of the Jordan Valley that was like the Garden of Eden and included the city of Sodom.

"I will give you this land as far as your eye can see," the Lord said to Abram. "Your descendants will be so numerous that they'll be hard to count." Then Abram moved west to Mamre, which is near Hebron, and built an altar there (Gen. 13).

Sometime later four chieftains from Mesopotamia came south, attacked five chieftains in the Jordan Valley, and took many captives, including Lot and his family and all their possessions. Hearing about it, Abram and his men went after those raiders, defeated them, and rescued the captives, including Lot and his family.

When Abram returned with the captives, Melchizedek, the king of Salem, joined by the king of Sodom, welcomed the captives back home and brought gifts of food and drink to Abram and his men out of gratitude for what they had done. The king of Salem was a worshipper of the God of heaven, as well as a priest. Greeting Abram, he said, "Bless you, and blessed be the God of heaven who delivered you from your enemies."

Abram responded by giving Melchizedek a tenth of all the spoils he had brought back with him, and the king of Salem accepted the tenth and thanked him. But the king of Sodom said, "Now just let me have my people, and keep the rest of the goods for yourself."

"As the Lord lives," Abram told him, "I will not accept even a sandal strap, because I don't want anyone to say afterward that he helped make Abram rich. I have not taken anything except food to feed my men" (Gen. 14).

The Covenant

After this the Lord spoke to Abram in a vision and said, "Don't be afraid. I will be your protection and will reward you for your faith in Me."

"Lord, what good will my reward be if I have no descendants to inherit the land You promised me?" Abram replied. "The only possible heir is my chief servant, Eliezer."

God said, "He will not inherit the land—your son will. Go outside and count the stars. That's how many descendants you will have." Abram believed God, and because of his faith in Him, the Lord considered him righteous.

"I called you out of Ur in the land of Babylon and promised to give you this land," God told him.

"How will I know that this land will be mine?" Abram asked.

"Go bring me a young cow, a goat, and a ram, plus a dove and a pigeon. Then do what I tell you to do."

Abram got the animals, slaughtered them, cut them in two (except the birds), and placed the halves opposite each other. Soon the vultures came, but Abram drove them away. After the sun had set, Abram fell asleep and dreamed that a strange darkness closed in around him. He was terrified.

"Don't be afraid, Abram," God said. "You will live to a good old age and will die in peace. Your descendants will be pilgrims and strangers in the land and during hard times they will go to Egypt to buy food. However, while they are there, they will be made slaves and be treated very cruelly. Four generations later I will deliver them, and they will come out with many possessions and inherit the land."

Then a smoking pot of fire and a burning torch passed between the animal pieces, and the Lord said to Abram, "I confirm My promise to give this land to your descendants from the borders of Egypt to the Euphrates River" (Gen. 15).

Sarai's Solution

Sarai couldn't have children, so she decided to let her servant Hagar have a baby for her. She talked to Abram about it, and they decided that it was the only way to have an heir and fulfill God's promise.

So Abram visited Hagar, and she became pregnant. As soon as she was sure she had conceived, her attitude toward Sarai changed. She felt superior to Sarai and refused to listen to her. When Sarai told Abram about it, he reassured her that the young woman's status had not changed—she would still be her servant. When Sarai reported to Hagar what Abram had said, the servant woman ran away.

23

The Lord was watching over Hagar and saw her stop to rest by a well. "Where are you going?" He asked her.

"I'm running away from Sarai."

"You need to go back to Sarai and quietly serve her," God said. "Your baby will be a boy, and I want you to name him Ishmael. He will have a hard life, but I will bless him."

"You are the God who sees and knows everything," she said, and she named the well El Roi, "the well of the One who sees and knows." Then she returned to Sarai, gave birth to a son, and named him Ishmael, as God had told her to. Abram was 86 when Ishmael was born (Gen. 16).

Name Change

Thirteen years later the Lord renewed His promise to Abram and said, "Continue doing what's right, and I will bless you with many descendants. You will be the father of many nations, so I am changing your name to Abraham. Even kings will be among your descendants.

"As a physical sign of this agreement, I want you to be circumcised, as well as all your men, and every 8-day-old baby boy. If the men or the parents refuse, you need to let them go.

"Also, I am changing Sarai's name to Sarah. She will conceive and have a son and become the mother of many nations."

When Abraham heard that, he laughed to himself and thought, *How can a man who is almost 100 years old with a 90-year-old wife have a baby?* Then he said to the Lord, "Let Ishmael be my heir."

"No, Sarah is going to have a baby, and I want you to name him Isaac. He will be your heir. Don't worry; I won't forget Ishmael. I will bless him, too, and he will be the father of a great nation. But I will fulfill My promise through Isaac. About this time next year Sarah will have a baby."

So Abraham went ahead and had all his men circumcised, including 13-year-old Ishmael (Gen. 17).

Visitors

Not long afterward, the Lord came to visit Abraham as he sat by his tent pitched among the terebinth trees of Mamre. From a distance Abraham saw three men standing under the trees. Running out to meet them, he bowed courteously and invited them to stop and have a bite to eat and to rest awhile. They accepted his invitation.

Abraham hurried to find Sarah and asked her to make some bread. Then he selected a young calf and told one of his servants to kill it and prepare some meat for his guests. When everything was ready, Abraham served the three travelers and stood by as they ate.

Then one of them asked, "Where is Sarah?"

"She's in the tent," Abraham answered.

"This time next year she will have a son," the man told him.

Hearing it, Sarah laughed to herself, thinking, *How can an old woman like me have a baby?*

"Why did Sarah laugh?" the visitor asked. "Is anything too hard for the Lord? This time next year she will have a baby."

Sarah came out and said, "I didn't laugh."

The stranger, who was actually the Lord, corrected her. "Yes, you did."

As the visitors got up to leave, Abraham decided to walk a little ways with them. The Lord said to the other two men, "Should we tell Abraham what we came for? After all, he will become the father of a great nation, and other nations will be blessed because of him. I know that he will continue to teach his family and servants to do what's right."

Then God turned to Abraham and told him how wicked Sodom and Gomorrah had become and that He and two angels had come personally to check things out before taking action.

The two angels continued on toward Sodom, leaving Abraham and the Lord to continue their conversation. "You aren't going to totally destroy the city and everyone in it, are You?" Abraham asked God. "Suppose there are 50 good people there. To destroy them wouldn't be right."

"If there are 50 good people there, for their sake I would spare the whole city," the Lord told him.

"What if there are 45?" Abraham continued.

"I would save the city for 45."

"What about 40?"

"Even for 40," God said.

Abraham pressed the issue: "What about 30 or even 20?"

"Even for 20."

Then Abraham asked one last time. "What about 10?"

"Yes, I would spare the city for just 10."

Then the Lord left, and Abraham went back to his tent (Gen. 18).

Angels and Lot

That same day the two angels went to Sodom and found Lot sitting by the city gate. When he saw the two strangers approaching, he stood up, greeted them, and invited them to his house.

"Thank you, but we'll spend the night in the city square."

But Lot insisted that they stay overnight at his home, so they finally agreed.

That evening, after he had fed them, someone knocked on the door.

After Lot opened it to see who it was, he saw a group of men, both young and old, standing outside. When he asked what he could do for them, they demanded, "Where are your guests? We want to welcome them by having a party and having sex with them."

"Please don't do that," Lot protested. "I have two daughters. Let me bring them out to you." He then reached back to go in and to close the door behind him.

"Get out of the way!" the men ordered. "Who made you our judge? You're not from around here, anyway. We're coming in!" Then the two angels pulled Lot back inside, and struck the men with blindness.

"Do you have other family members in the city?" they asked Lot. "If you do, you need to warn them to get out of the city, because the Lord sent us here to destroy it."

Quickly Lot went and told his other daughters and sons-in-law what had happened and begged them to flee the city with him, but they only laughed at his fears. Just before daylight Lot returned home, alone. Then the angels urged him to hurry, take his wife and the two daughters still at home, and leave, but Lot hesitated. So the angels grabbed the four of them by the hand and led them out of the city.

Once beyond the city walls, one of the angels said, "Run for your lives! Head for the hills so that you won't be destroyed. And don't look back!"

"We don't know how to survive in the mountains," Lot protested. "Please let us go to the little town of Zoar, which is close by."

"All right, but hurry! I can't do anything until you're safe."

As soon as Lot and his family reached Zoar, fire flashed down from heaven and destroyed Sodom, nearby cities, and everything in the valley. Lot's wife longingly looked back at Sodom, and as she did, her body turned into a pillar of salt.

That same morning Abraham hurried to where he had been with the Lord, and as he looked toward Sodom, he saw the whole valley on fire and a huge cloud of smoke rising into the sky as if coming from a furnace.

When the Lord destroyed Sodom and Gomorrah, He had kept Abraham's concern for Lot's safety in mind, and that was one reason among others that He rescued him (Gen. 19:1-29).

Lot's Descendants

Afraid to stay in Zoar, Lot took his two daughters and went up into the mountains to live. One day the older daughter said to her younger sister, "There are no men up here. How can we ever have children and preserve our father's line? I tell you what. Let's get Father drunk, and I'll sleep with him tonight. Tomorrow we'll get him drunk again, and then you can sleep with him." The younger daughter agreed, and they both became pregnant. Each time Lot was so drunk that he wasn't fully awake and didn't know when his daughters came and when they left.

The older daughter named her baby Moab, who became the father of the Moabites. The younger daughter named her baby Ben-ammi, who became the father of the Ammonites. Both groups became enemies of Israel (Gen. 19:30-38).

God Protects Sarah

Abraham moved from Mamre south into Philistia, just beyond Gaza. He told the local people that Sarah was his sister. Their king, attracted by Sarah's beauty, brought her to the palace. That night God spoke to him in a dream, saying, "If you touch that woman, you'll die. She's Abraham's wife."

"But he told me she was his sister," Abimelech protested, "and she said that he was her brother!"

"I know you brought her to your palace ignorantly. That's why I'm stopping you from sinning, so give Abraham back his wife."

First thing in the morning, the king told his servants everything that God had said. Then he summoned Abraham and asked him, "Why did you do this to me?"

"Because I thought you might kill me for her," Abraham said. "She really is my half sister, and I had asked her to tell you that I'm her brother."

So the king gave Sarah back to Abraham along with presents of sheep, cattle, servants, and a thousand pieces of silver. Then he added, "You may stay in our country if you like. There's plenty of room."

Now the Lord had stopped Abimelech and his wife from having children. So Abraham prayed for them and for the king's household, and the Lord answered Abraham's prayer and healed Abimelech and his wife and their servants (Gen. 20).

Isaac

About this time Sarah became pregnant, just as God had promised she would. She named her son Isaac, which means "joy and laughter," because God had brought joy to her heart. "Just think!" she said, "Who ever heard of an old woman nursing a baby?" Abraham was about 100 years old at this time, and Sarah was 90.

When Isaac was 8 days old, Abraham had him circumcised. Then when Isaac was a young child, he was weaned, and Abraham and Sarah celebrated the occasion by holding a great feast.

Hagar's son, Ishmael, was a teenager when Isaac was weaned. As Isaac grew, Ishmael kept making fun of him. Day after day Sarah saw what was happening, and finally she said to Abraham, "You need to send Hagar and her son away. If they stay, things will only get worse."

The demand hurt Abraham, but the Lord said to him, "Listen to your wife, and don't worry about Ishmael. I will watch over him and bless him because he is your son."

So Abraham talked with Hagar and her son, gave them water and provisions, and sent them on their way to Egypt.

When the food and water ran out, Hagar stopped to rest by some trees and told Ishmael to wait there while she went in search of water. Going off a little ways, she sat down and cried. She said to herself, "I can't stand to see my son die, so it's better if we die separately."

Ishmael was crying also, but God saw their tears and sent an angel to help them.

The angel said to Hagar, "Don't worry. God knows where the boy is and has heard him crying. Go back and comfort him. The Lord will make a great nation of him."

Then the angel showed Hagar a source of water, and she filled her containers, went back to Ishmael, and told him what the angel had said. So they decided to stay in the area, and God blessed the boy, who grew up to be a skillful hunter. When he was old enough to marry, Hagar found a girl from Egypt to be his wife (Gen. 21:1-21).

Peace Treaty

About this time Abimelech and his army commander went to see Abraham. "We know that God is with you," they said to him. "Let's make a peace treaty so our descendants won't think we're enemies and start fighting."

Abraham agreed. "Good idea, but there is one thing we need to settle first. Your men took over the well my servants dug."

"Why didn't you tell me? I'll stop that right now."

So Abraham gave the king sheep and cattle as a sign of friendship, and they both signed the treaty. Then Abraham gave Abimelech an additional seven lambs. "What are these for?" the king asked.

"Take them as a sign that my servants dug this well."

After they concluded their treaty, Abimelech and his military leader returned home.

Naming the well "Beersheba," meaning "the well of oath," Abraham planted a special tree by the well as a reminder of the agreement. He stayed in the area for some time, serving and worshipping the Lord (Gen. 21:22-34).

Abraham Tested

When Isaac was a young man, God tested Abraham's faith and said to him, "Take your only son, Isaac, whom you love so much, and go to Mount Moriah, and offer him as a sacrifice."

Abraham couldn't imagine that God would ask him to do this! But he got up early, saddled his donkey, loaded it with wood, and, together with Isaac and two young servants, headed for Mount Moriah. It took three days to get there. Abraham struggled to grasp God's command, but finally told himself that if he understood the Lord's promise correctly that he would have descendants, God would have to raise Isaac from the dead. How else could He fulfill His promise?

When they reached Mount Moriah, Abraham told the young servants to stay with the donkey while he and Isaac went up the mountain to worship. Then he put the wood on Isaac's back, took the knife, and in a container carried the hot coals that he would use to start the fire.

As they walked up the mountain, Isaac asked, "Father, we have the hot coals and the wood, but where is the lamb?"

"The Lord will provide His own lamb," Abraham said. So they continued up the mountain.

When they arrived at the top, they built a low stone altar and placed the wood on it. Then Abraham told Isaac of God's plan, and Isaac carefully listened to what his father was saying. Finally he agreed to be the sacrifice. He let his father tie his hands, and he submissively laid down on the altar.

As Abraham raised the knife to sacrifice his son, suddenly a voice from heaven cried out, "Abraham! Abraham!"

"I'm here, Lord!"

"Don't touch the young man! You have shown that you would hold nothing back from Me, not even your own son."

Then, as Abraham lifted his gaze, he saw a ram caught by its horns in a thorn bush. So he took the ram and offered it as a sacrifice in place of Isaac. He named the place Jehovah Jireh, meaning "the Lord will provide."

The voice from heaven spoke again: "I swear by My own name, because you were willing to sacrifice your only son, I will bless you and multiply your descendants so that they will be as difficult to count as the stars in the sky or the grains of sand on the shore. All nations will be blessed because of you."

Then Abraham and his son went down the mountain and, together with the two servants, returned to Beersheba (Gen. 22:1-19).

Sarah Dies

Sarah was 127 years old when she died in Hebron in the land of Canaan. Abraham grieved greatly at losing Sarah.

CHOSEN: Genesis Through Deuteronomy

Then he went and spoke to the local Canaanites and said, "I'm a foreigner in your country, but you have been so kind to let me settle here. Please sell me a piece of property as a burial place for Sarah, my wife."

"You are a mighty leader among us," they replied. "Pick the place you want."

When he selected a spot, the owner said to Abraham, "I'll give it to you."

"No, let me buy it from you," Abraham told him.

"It's worth 400 pieces of silver," the man said, "but your friendship is worth more than that."

Abraham counted out 400 pieces of silver, and the landowner accepted them.

The property included a field with trees and a cave. So Abraham buried Sarah in the cave, which was part of the field of Machpelah, near Mamre (Gen. 23).

Isaac Marries

Abraham was getting up in years and was worried about Isaac not having a wife. So he called in his most trusted servant and said, "I don't want Isaac to marry one of the Canaanite girls. Promise me that you'll go back to my country and find a wife for him from among my relatives. Don't take Isaac with you—God will help you. If you can't find a girl who will come with you, then I'll release you from your responsibility."

The servant agreed, and a few days later he took 10 camels and some other servants and headed for the city of Nahor. When he got there, he stopped by a well and prayed that God would direct things so that when the women came to draw water, the one to be Isaac's wife would be one of them and would offer him a drink and water his camels. He didn't have to wait long before Rebekah came along and did just that. She was a beautiful girl.

When she had finished watering the camels, Abraham's servant thanked her and gave her a ring and two bracelets. Then he asked, "Whose daughter are you?"

"My father is Bethuel," she said, "and my grandfather is Nahor."

The servant couldn't believe it! Bowing to the ground, he thanked the Lord for leading him to Abraham's family so quickly. Then he asked Rebekah if he could stay at their house overnight. Rebekah ran home to ask her family.

When her brother, Laban, saw the rings and bracelets that she showed him and heard that the man was Abraham's servant, he ran to the well to invite him home. The servant accepted the invitation, and when they got there, he and his men first unloaded the camels and fed them, and then they all went in to have something to eat.

30

"Let me tell you why I'm here," Abraham's servant began. "The Lord has blessed Abraham with large flocks and herds and many servants. He has a son named Isaac, who is of marriageable age, so Abraham asked me to come here to find a wife for Isaac and assured me that God would help me." Then he told the family how he had prayed and about everything that had happened at the well.

Rebekah's father and brother listened carefully and said, "This is of the Lord, but it's not up to us to say one way or the other whether Rebekah should marry Isaac—it's her decision. If she wants to go with you, we won't stand in her way."

Then Abraham's servant asked Rebekah, and she agreed to go. Only then did he and his men sit down to eat.

The next morning the servant was ready to start back home, but Rebekah's mother and brother said, "Let her stay at home for 10 more days, and then she can go."

"Please don't delay me after the Lord has made things so evident," the servant replied.

"Let's ask Rebekah," they responded.

"I would like to go now," she told them.

So they gave her the family's blessing and said, "May you become the mother of thousands, and may your descendants always overcome their enemies!"

So they left, and when they neared Abraham's home, it so happened that Isaac had gone out in the field to pray. As he looked off in the distance, he saw camels approaching. Rebekah then noticed a man in the field coming toward them. Getting off the camel, she asked who it was. Abraham's servant told her it was Isaac, so she quickly took a veil and, as the custom was, covered her face.

Then the servant told Isaac everything that had happened and introduced him to Rebekah. Isaac loved her and later brought her into his mother's tent, and they became husband and wife. With Rebekah by his side, Isaac was finally comforted after his mother's death (Gen. 24).

Abraham Dies

After Sarah died, Abraham married again and had six more sons, but he willed everything to Isaac. However, he did give large gifts of sheep and cattle to his other sons and asked them to move to another part of the country and settle there.

Abraham was 175 years old when he died. Isaac and Ishmael talked it over and decided to bury their father in the cave of Machpelah next to Sarah. And the Lord blessed Isaac as He had blessed Abraham (Gen. 25:1-11).

three

Isaac and Jacob

Isaac was 40 years old when he married Rebekah. He prayed earnestly for children, and the Lord heard his prayer. Rebekah became pregnant with twins, two boys who were kicking extremely hard inside of her, so she asked the Lord about it.

"They represent two rival people," God explained. "The one who comes out first will serve the second one, who will be the stronger."

Isaac was 60 years old at the time their two boys were born. They named the first one Esau and the second one Jacob. Esau grew up loving the outdoors and became a skillful hunter. Jacob was quieter and preferred to stay near home to take care of the flocks and herds. Isaac had more of a liking for Esau, and Rebekah for Jacob.

One day Esau came back from hunting terribly hungry. Although he had searched for game all day, he had found nothing. When he saw Jacob cooking a pot of lentils and smelled the baking bread, he said, "I'm starved! Let me have some of that red stuff and that fresh bread."

"Sure, if you'll let me have your birthright as spiritual leader of the family," Jacob replied.

"I couldn't care less for that. If you want it, you can have it! Just give me something to eat!"

"Take an oath to confirm it," Jacob insisted.

Esau took an oath, and Jacob gave him all he wanted to eat. After he had satisfied his hunger, Esau went away happy, not the least concerned about the spiritual birthright that he had just given away (Gen. 25:20-34).

Isaac and Abimelech

About this time a famine struck that part of the country, much as it had been in the days of Abraham. So Isaac took his family south to Gerar as his father had done.

When the men of the area asked him about Rebekah (because she was very beautiful), Isaac told them she was his sister, because he didn't want to be killed. Not long afterward, Abimelech, the local king, happened to look out the window and saw Isaac hugging and stroking Rebekah. So he called him in and said, "This woman is your wife! Why did you say she was your sister?"

"I was afraid the men might kill me to get her, Isaac replied." Then the king told his men that anyone who touched Isaac or his wife would be killed.

The Lord continued to bless Isaac with flocks and herds, as he had done his father, Abraham. The local people had been jealous of Abraham, and when he died, they plugged up all the wells that he had dug. Isaac unplugged one of the wells, but doing so created a lot of bad feelings, and the people claimed that it was theirs. Isaac let them have that well and dug a new one, but they argued about that one, too. Again he allowed them to seize it and dug a second well, but the same thing happened once more. So he decided to leave the valley.

Isaac decided to move to Beersheba. There the Lord spoke to him in a dream and said, "Don't be afraid. I am with you, as I was with Abraham, your father. I will bless you, as I promised him I would." In the morning Isaac built an altar to the Lord and thanked Him for His protection.

Then Abimelech and his army commander went to see Isaac. Surprised, Isaac asked the ruler, "Why did you come to see me after you told me to leave?"

"We know that God is with you, as He was with your father," the king answered, "so we came to make the same agreement with you that we made with him."

So Isaac prepared a feast for his guests, and the next morning they sealed their peace agreement with an oath and parted as friends.

Later that same day Isaac's servants told him they had dug a well and found water. He gave the new well the same name Abraham had given the old one—Shebah, meaning "the well of the oath," and that's how the future city of Beersheba got its name (Gen. 26:1–33).

Isaac and Jacob

When Isaac was old, he said to Esau, "Son, I don't know how much longer I'll live. I'm having all kinds of problems and am almost blind. Hunt some wild game for me, and make that tasty dish that I like. Then let's eat together, and I'll give you the family blessing before I die."

Rebekah overheard them and told Jacob, "Your father wants to give Esau the family blessing. Listen to me. Esau has just gone out hunting, and while he's gone, we can prepare the food your father likes, and he'll then give you the blessing when you bring it to him."

"I'm not so sure about that," Jacob objected. "Esau has lots of hair on his body, and I don't. Father knows the difference even though he can't see well, and when he realizes that I'm trying to deceive him, he'll put a curse on me."

"If he does, let the curse fall on me," his mother answered.

So Jacob brought in two baby goats, and Rebekah made Isaac's favorite dish. Then she took the goatskin and put it around Jacob's arms and neck and told him to take the dish to his father. At first Jacob hesitated, but finally did what his mother said. He went in to see his father and said, "Father, it's me, Esau. Here's your favorite dish."

"Son, how did you do all this so fast?" Isaac asked in surprise.

"God helped me."

"Come here." Isaac felt Jacob's arms and neck and was puzzled. "You feel and smell like Esau, but your voice sounds like Jacob's. Are you really Esau?"

"I am."

So they ate together, then Isaac hugged his son and gave him the family blessing, saying, "May the blessings of Abraham be yours. May you have large herds and flocks, plenty of grain, and many servants. May everyone look up to you, and may nations bow before you. Cursed be those who curse you, and blessed be those who bless you."

As soon as Jacob left, Esau returned from hunting, prepared his father's favorite meal, and took it in to him. When Esau came in, Isaac said, "Who are you?"

"I'm Esau, your son."

Starting to shake all over, Isaac said, "Someone brought me my favorite dish and said he was Esau, and I gave him the family blessing!"

When Esau heard this, he broke down and cried. "Father, please bless me, too," he pleaded.

"There's only one family blessing," Isaac explained. "It must have been Jacob who deceived me, and I gave it to him."

"He's deceived me twice! First he took away my birthright, and now he's taken the family blessing! But at least bless me!"

So Isaac gave Esau a general blessing: "The Lord will be with you. The open field will be your home, and you will live by the sword. You will be subject to the influence of your brother, but you will break his hold on you and be free."

Esau now vowed that after Isaac died, he would kill Jacob. Word got back to Rebekah, and she said to Jacob, "You need to go to Haran to your uncle Laban's house and stay there until your brother cools down. I'll send word when it's safe for you to come back."

Next she went to talk to Isaac. "Esau has married a couple local girls, and they're giving me no end of trouble," she said. "Jacob must not stay here and marry a Canaanite."

So Isaac called Jacob in, did not mention the deception, but said, "I want you to visit your mother's brother, Laban, to find a wife there. You must not marry a Canaanite." Then he blessed him, saying, "May the God of heaven watch over you and multiply your descendants. May the blessing of Abraham be yours, and may you inherit the land that God promised."

When Esau found out that his marriages to Canaanite women disturbed his parents, he then married one of Ishmael's daughters also (Gen. 27:1-28:9).

Jacob at Bethel

Jacob said goodbye to his mother, left Beersheba, and headed for Haran. By the time he reached Bethel he was very tired. Finding a flat stone, he used it for a pillow and fell sound asleep. During the night he had a dream. He saw a stairway leading from earth to heaven, with angels going up and down on it. At the top stood the Lord, who said, "I am the God of Abraham and Isaac. I will give you and your descendants the land on which you're sleeping. Through your seed all nations will be blessed. I will be with you wherever you go and will bring you safely back home."

Then Jacob woke up and said, "The Lord is in this place! It's like the house of God, the gate of heaven!" And he named it Bethel, which means "house of God," though the place was formerly called Luz. Then Jacob took an oath and said, "If God will take care of me and bring me back home in peace, the Lord will always be my God, and I will surely give Him a tenth of all my increase" (Gen. 28:10-22).

Jacob and Rachel

After weeks of travel, Jacob finally reached the city of Haran. At the outskirts of the city he saw a well and flocks of sheep waiting to be watered. He asked the shepherds where they came from, and some of them said, "Haran."

"Do you know Laban?"

"Yes, we do. There comes his daughter Rachel with her flock."

"Why aren't you watering your sheep? It's time to get them out to pasture."

"We don't roll away the stone until we're all here."

While they were talking, Rachel arrived with her flock. Jacob told her that he was the grandson of Abraham and son of Rebekah, gave her a hug, and cried. When the men heard that, they let Jacob roll away the stone and water Rachel's sheep first. Meanwhile, she ran home and told her father what had happened. Laban then went to the well to meet Jacob, kissed him on both cheeks, and invited him home.

After catching up on all the family news, Laban asked Jacob to stay with him, offering him the job of caring for his flocks and herds, which his nephew accepted.

Laban had two daughters, Leah and Rachel, but Jacob loved Rachel. So he said to Laban, "I have nothing to guarantee your daughter a secure future. But I'll work for you for seven years if you promise to let me marry Rachel."

"I'd rather have you marry her than have her marry someone else."

So Jacob labored for Laban and at the end of the seven years asked him for Rachel. By this time he had flocks and herds of his own. Laban agreed and made plans for the wedding. But that evening he brought Leah, fully veiled, to Jacob instead. As a wedding present, her father gave her a maid of her own.

The next morning when Jacob got up, he realized that he had slept with Leah. He ran to his father-in-law and said angrily, "I asked you for Rachel, not Leah!"

"It's the custom here that the younger daughter can't marry until the older one gets married," Laban argued. "Wait until the wedding week is over, and you can have Rachel, too, if you promise to work for me for another seven years."

Jacob agreed to Laban's terms—what else could he do? When the week ended, Laban held another feast and brought in Rachel. As a wedding present, he also gave her a maidservant.

Jacob loved Rachel more than he did Leah and didn't mind working for Laban another seven years for her (Gen. 29:1-30).

Jacob's Children

The Lord noticed that Jacob loved Rachel more than he did Leah, so He blessed Leah, and she began having children. Her firstborn was Reuben, the second Simeon, the third Levi, and the fourth Judah. Then it seemed that she couldn't have any more.

Jealous of Leah and her many children, Rachel blamed Jacob for her inability to become pregnant. Becoming angry, he snapped, "Don't blame me! I'm not God!" Then Rachel urged him to sleep with her maid so that her servant could have children for her. The maid got pregnant and gave Rachel a son, whom she named Dan. When the woman became pregnant again, Rachel named that son Naphtali.

When Leah saw that, she urged Jacob to sleep with *her* maid. The woman conceived and bore Leah a son, whom she named Gad. Soon the servant had a second child, and Leah named the boy Asher.

This whole thing created a lot of rivalry between the two sisters, each one wanting to have the most children. Then Leah got pregnant with Issachar and then Zebulun. So Leah bore Jacob six sons, plus two from her maid. She also had a daughter named Dinah.

Then God answered Rachel's prayer, and she conceived and had a son of her own, whom she named Joseph. Rachel believed she would have another son, and later she did. So Rachel would give Jacob two sons, plus two from her maid (Gen. 29:31-30:24).

Jacob Returns Home

After Rachel gave birth to Joseph, Jacob decided to return home. He told Laban his plans, but his uncle protested, "No, don't go! The Lord has blessed me through you. Name your wages, and I'll pay whatever you ask."

"It's not wages that I need so much as future security for my growing family. If you will let me have the speckled and spotted sheep and goats and the dark-colored lambs for my wages, I'll stay."

Laban agreed, so he went out to the field and separated out the type of animals that Jacob had asked for and told his sons to take them three days' walk away to prevent interbreeding with the rest of Laban's flocks and herds.

But Laban's flocks and herds kept producing more multicolored off-spring than ever before, and Jacob made sure that they mated with each other and not with the others. It wasn't long before Jacob had huge flocks and herds, and his animals were stronger and healthier than Laban's.

Word got back to Jacob that Laban's sons were accusing him of taking away their father's wealth. It made Laban even less friendly toward Jacob than he had been before.

Then the Lord said to Jacob, "It's time for you to go back home—I'll be with you." Jacob sent word to Leah and Rachel to meet him out in the field, because he needed to talk to them. When they arrived, he said, "I've worked hard for your father all these years, yet he has cheated me and lowered my wages 10 times. I had a dream and the Lord said, 'I made the multicolored animals produce more, because I saw what Laban has been doing to you. I spoke to you at Bethel and promised to bring you back home. Now is the time.'"

"There's nothing for us here," Jacob's wives said to him, "and our father treats us as if we were foreigners. What God has done for you belongs to us, so let's do what He says."

While Laban and his sons were out in the field shearing their sheep, Rachel took her father's household idols without Jacob's knowledge to make up for her father's dishonesty. Quickly Jacob left with his family, animals, and servants. On his way he crossed the Euphrates River and headed for home (Gen. 30:25-31:21).

Laban Pursues Jacob

Three days later Laban heard what had happened, so he took his men and went after Jacob to bring him back. Seven days later they caught up with him and camped a short distance away. That night God spoke to Laban in a dream and said, "Be careful what you say to Jacob."

The next morning Laban and his men entered Jacob's camp, and Laban said to Jacob, "Why did you leave in such a hurry and not even let me know? Why all this secrecy? We could have had a farewell feast, and at least I could have said goodbye to my daughters and grandchildren. What you did was not very smart. I have enough men to force you to come back with me, but God spoke to me in a dream last night and told me not to do it. I know you're in a hurry to get back home, but why did you have to steal my gods?"

"I left in a hurry, because I was afraid you'd threaten to take Leah and Rachel away from me unless I stayed," Jacob explained. "But why would I steal your gods? Search the whole camp, and if you find them, I'll order the person who took them to be killed. I'll let your own men search the camp, and you and I will go with them to make sure they do a good job." Jacob didn't know that Rachel had stolen the idols.

Laban and his men searched all the family tents, and the last one was Rachel's. She was sitting on a cushion draped over a camel's saddle with the idols underneath, and she excused herself for not getting up because of her monthly period. Respecting her privacy, Laban carefully searched the rest of the tent but found nothing.

Then Jacob got angry. "What have I done to make you come after me like this? I worked for you for 20 years and never cheated you! Yet you cheated me by lowering my wages 10 times, and when wild animals stole or killed sheep or goats, you took it out of my pay. I slept in the field at night, enduring the cold and heat to protect your flocks and herds. I worked 14 years for your daughters and six more years for you. If God hadn't intervened, you would have sent me away empty-handed. That's why He rebuked you last night."

"Aren't these my daughters and grandchildren that you have?" his uncle retorted. "Let's make a peace treaty." Jacob agreed and set up a large stone to mark the spot. Then he asked his family to get some more stones and pile them up to make a little monument.

After they had eaten together, Laban said, "Let this pile of stones be a sign of peace between us. May the Lord watch over us while we are absent from one another. I will not cross over to you, and you won't cross over to me. If you are not faithful to my daughters and grandchildren, God will know about it. Let the God of Abraham be our judge." They named the pile of stones Mizpah, meaning "little watchtower."

Going up a nearby hill, Jacob offered a sacrifice to the Lord, then invited his family and Laban to join him in a ceremonial feast. They camped there all night, and in the morning Laban blessed his daughters and grandchildren, hugged and kissed them, and said goodbye (Gen. 31:22-55).

A New Name

After Jacob said goodbye to Laban, he broke camp and headed for home. On the way God let Jacob see the angels that He had sent to protect him. It reminded him of his experience at Bethel 20 years before when he left home.

Then Jacob sent messengers ahead to his brother, Esau, to let him know he was coming. "Tell Esau, 'Your servant Jacob is on his way from Uncle Laban's, together with his wives and children and large flocks and herds. May he find favor in your sight.'"

When the messengers returned, they told Jacob that Esau had with him 400 armed men. When Jacob heard that, he remembered Esau's threat to kill him and feared for his life. So he separated his family and animals into two groups, thinking that if his brother attacked one of them, the others could get away.

"O Lord God of Abraham and Isaac," he prayed, "You told me to return home. I'm not worthy of Your mercy and kindness. Twenty years ago when I crossed the Jordan River, I was alone. Now look at my large family. You've blessed me more than I deserve, but I'm scared. Esau is coming to kill me, and who knows what he'll do to my family! You promised that my descendants would be as numerous as the grains of sand on the seashore. Please help me!"

In the morning Jacob decided to send his brother, Esau, a present of three batches of animals from his herds and flocks. He instructed the servants with the first one, "If Esau asks you where you're going, tell him that these animals are a present to him from Jacob and that I'm not far behind you." He said the same thing to those with the other two groups, hoping it might work.

Before dark he took his family across the Jabbok Brook and set up camp. Then he went back across to spend the night alone in prayer. In the morning hours, while it was still dark, someone came quietly and attacked him. Jacob fought with all his strength to save his life, but after hours of wrestling and struggling, he couldn't get rid of the man. Then at the first light of day, the person touched Jacob's hip, throwing it out of joint. Instantly, Jacob knew that the individual was someone sent from God—maybe an angel—but Jacob would not let go of him.

"Stop holding on to me!" the person commanded.

"I won't let you go unless you bless me!" Jacob insisted.

"What's your name?"

"Jacob."

"I'm changing your name to Israel, because you have wrestled with me and would not let go."

"What is your name?" Jacob countered.

"Why do you need to know?" Then he blessed Jacob and disappeared.

"I have seen God, and I'm still alive!" Jacob said to himself. So he called the place Penuel, meaning "the face of God." As the sun came up, Jacob limped back across the brook, with the help of his shepherd's staff, and into the camp to his family.

To this day his descendants will not eat the muscle next to the hip of any animal, out of respect for Jacob (Gen. 32).

Jacob Meets Esau

Breaking camp, Jacob divided his family into groups around each of the mothers, and slowly and painfully led the way to meet Esau. When he saw his brother, he bowed for a total of seven times as he got closer and closer. When Esau recognized him, he ran to meet Jacob, hugging him and kissing him on both cheeks, and they both cried.

Then Esau looked around and said, "Who are all these people?"

"This is my family." Each of the maids came with their children and bowed before Esau, followed by Leah and Rachel and their children.

"Why did you send me these groups of animals?" Esau asked.

"I sent them to you as presents, hoping you would accept me back as your brother."

"Of course I will! But keep what you have. I have enough."

"No, my brother. I am so glad to see you again and to know that you have accepted me that I want you to take these gifts as an expression of my appreciation for your kindness." At Jacob's urging, Esau finally accepted the gifts.

"Come, my brother," Esau said finally, "let's head for home. I'll lead the way."

"Please, my family can't travel as fast as your men can. Besides that, some animals are still nursing. To drive them hard would kill them. Go on ahead, and we'll get there soon."

"Well, then, let some of my men remain with you."

"There's no need for that, but thank you for your kind offer."

So Esau went ahead and Jacob followed. When Jacob got to Shechem, he bought a piece of land and built an altar. He named the altar El Elohe Israel as a memorial to the God of Israel who had brought him back home (Gen. 33).

Esau's Family

After Jacob returned, Esau moved out of the area to give his brother room for his flocks and herds. With his three wives and children, Esau then settled in the land of Edom, and that's why his descendants are called Edomites.

They became so numerous that they divided themselves into tribes. Among Esau's descendants were some powerful chiefs and later powerful rulers, known as the "kings of Edom" (Gen. 36).

Dinah

When Leah's daughter, Dinah, went to meet the young women of the land, and Shechem, the local prince, saw how beautiful Dinah was, he took her home and forced her to sleep with him. He fell in love with her and asked his father, Hamor, to get permission from Jacob to marry her.

Jacob heard what had happened and decided to tell Dinah's brothers of the prince's request when they were all together. In the meantime, King Hamor came to see Jacob and said, "My son Shechem is in love with your daughter and would like to marry her. Personally, I think that would be a good idea, for it would help both of us. We could intermarry and become a larger, stronger people."

Then Shechem, who was with his father, spoke up and said to Jacob and Dinah's brothers, who had come to take part in the discussion, "Ask what family gift I should bring, and I'll be glad to do it. Just let me marry her!"

Because he had forced their sister to sleep with him, Dinah's brothers came up with a plan to punish the prince. "Before we give our permission and become one people," they said, "you and your men need to be circumcised. Then we will go ahead with marriage."

Hamor and his son accepted their proposition and went back to talk to the men of the little city. They told them of Shechem's love for Dinah and the plan for intermarriage to become a more powerful people. So the men agreed to be circumcised.

Three days later, while the men were still recovering, Simeon and Levi took their swords, went into the little city, and killed all the adult males, including King Hamor and his son Shechem. Then they went into Shechem's house to get Dinah to bring her back home. Also, they took all the flocks and herds of the people as well as their women and children and made them work for them.

When Jacob heard what they had done, he couldn't believe it. He called Simeon and Levi in and said, "What have you two done! Have you gone mad! You've made the family name stink among the people in this country. I wouldn't be surprised if they all got together to attack and kill us!"

"Are you saying we should have overlooked what Shechem did to Dinah?" Simeon and Levi demanded (Gen. 34).

Jacob Moves

Then God said to Jacob, "Move back to Bethel, build an altar, and worship Me there." Jacob told his family what God had said and reminded them why Bethel was such a special place of worship. He asked them to get rid of their little idols and jewelry and prepare to go. So they gave Jacob all their little gods, along with their earrings and jewelry. After he buried them by a large terebinth tree near the town of Shechem, they all left for Bethel. The people of the country did not attack Jacob, because they were afraid of his God.

When Jacob and his family reached Bethel, he built an altar there and named it El Bethel, meaning "an altar to the God of Bethel." Years ago that's where he had seen the stairway to heaven and had heard God speaking to him.

Here is where Deborah, his mother Rebekah's nurse, died, and Jacob buried her by a terebinth tree, which the people named "The Terebinth of Weeping."

Then God spoke to Jacob and said, "Remember that your name is not Jacob, but Israel. You will be fruitful and multiply and become a great nation. Even kings will be among your descendants, and the land I promised Abraham I will give to you."

So the altar Jacob built for a place to worship also became a memorial of God's promise to him. He poured oil and wine on the altar and offered sacrifices to the God of Bethel (Gen. 35:1-15).

Rachel Dies

From Bethel, Jacob decided to move to Ephrath. When they got as far as Bethlehem, Rachel went into labor and gave birth to a son. Complications set in, and as she was dying, she named her baby Ben-Oni, "Son of Sorrow," but Jacob renamed him Benjamin, "Son of the Right Hand."

Heartbroken, Jacob buried Rachel and set up a grave marker for her, which was there for years to come. Then he decided to settle with his 12 sons in the area between Bethlehem and Hebron (Gen. 35:16-26).

Isaac Dies

Jacob's father, Isaac, was 180 years old when he died. So Jacob and Esau went back to Mamre, where Abraham had lived, to bury him there. Then each of them returned to their families (Gen. 35:27-29).

four

Joseph

Jacob continued living in Canaan, where Abraham and Isaac had been. All his sons were grown and had families of their own, except Joseph and his younger brother, Benjamin, who still remained at home. Joseph was 17 years old, and Jacob loved him more than all his other sons. He gave Joseph a long-sleeved, multicolored tunic that, together with all the other attention Jacob gave him, made his brothers jealous.

One day Joseph said to his brothers, "I had a dream last night, and in it I saw 12 bundles of freshly harvested wheat. Suddenly my bundle stood up, and yours circled around it and bowed to it."

When his brothers heard this, they said, "Does this mean you're better than we are?" and they began to hate him.

Later he had another dream and told his father and brothers, "Last night I had a dream, and in it I saw the sun, the moon, and 11 stars bow to me."

Jacob rebuked him. "Do you think the whole family should bow down to you?"

So Joseph's brothers hated him even more, but Jacob never forgot that dream.

Not long afterward, his brothers took their flocks and herds to the area near Shechem for better grazing. As time passed and Jacob hadn't heard from his sons, he began to worry about them. So he sent Joseph to find out if anything had happened to his brothers. When Joseph got to Shechem and didn't find them, someone told him that they had moved their flocks and herds to Dothan, so Joseph went there.

When his brothers saw him approaching, they said, "Here comes the dreamer! We ought to kill him and tell Father a wild beast did it."

"Don't get any such ideas!" Reuben, the oldest, said. "Leave him alone!" Reuben intended to rescue Joseph and then take him back home.

As Joseph entered the brothers' camp, they grabbed him, ripped his

43

special tunic off, and threw him into a dry well. Then they sat down to eat.

While they were eating, a group of Ishmaelite merchants passed on their way to Egypt. Judah decided to save his brother, so he said, "Let's not kill Joseph—let's sell him!"

The brothers, with Judah's help, pulled Joseph out of the well and sold him for 20 pieces of silver.

When Reuben returned to camp and found that the others had sold Joseph, he tore his robe as a sign of grief and wept.

Then the brothers took Joseph's colored tunic, dipped it in blood, brought it to Jacob, and said, "We found this on the way home. Is this Joseph's tunic?"

Jacob looked at it and cried out, "It is! A wild animal killed him!" He tore his robe in grief, put on sackcloth, and mourned for Joseph for days. His sons tried to comfort him, but nothing could console Jacob. "I miss Joseph so much," he sobbed. "It will take me to my grave," and he continued grieving (Gen. 37:1–38:30).

Joseph in Egypt

When the Ishmaelite caravan arrived in Egypt, it sold Joseph to Potiphar, the captain of the royal guards. The Lord didn't forget Joseph but blessed him in all he did. As time went on, Potiphar noticed how dependable Joseph was in carrying out his responsibilities. The royal officer had no doubt in his mind that the Lord was with Joseph, so he put him in charge of everything he owned.

Joseph was a good-looking young man, so one day Potiphar's wife tried to seduce him. But he refused her advances and said, "My master trusts me, so how can I turn against him and also sin against God!" Although she kept tempting him, he always gave her the same answer.

One day Joseph went into Potiphar's house to do his work, and all the servants were gone. It seemed strange to him, but he went on about his duties. Then Potiphar's wife came in and tempted Joseph again. When he wouldn't respond, she grabbed his tunic and said, "Come, let's make love together!" Twisting out of his tunic, he ran from the house.

Then she screamed, "Come! Look at what this Hebrew slave tried to do to me! He took off his tunic and wanted to have sex with me!" The servants raced back into the house, but Joseph was already gone.

When Potiphar came home, his wife showed him Joseph's tunic and accused him of trying to rape her. Potiphar didn't believe his wife, but for the sake of his servants and their faith in his wife's honesty, he had no choice but to have Joseph arrested and thrown into prison.

In spite of this, Joseph did not let go of God, and the Lord blessed him.

Joseph was a model prisoner, and before long, the warden learned he could trust Joseph, and he put him in charge of the whole prison (Gen. 39).

Dreams

One day the royal butler and then the royal baker made the king angry, and he put them in prison. The warden assigned Joseph to care for their needs. Both men had a dream that really bothered them, so when Joseph came to see them in the morning, he asked why they looked so worried.

"Each of us had a dream last night," they explained, "and we're really concerned about what they mean, but who can interpret them for us?"

"God can," Joseph told them. "Tell me the dreams, and He will let us know what they mean."

"In my dream," the butler began, "I saw a grapevine with three branches bloom, develop clusters, and then produce grapes. I took the grapes and squeezed them into Pharaoh's cup and gave it to him."

"The three branches are three days," Joseph said. "In three days Pharaoh will take you out of prison and give you your job back. When that happens, say a kind word for me, because I'm a Hebrew who was sold as a slave and then falsely accused of hurting someone. I don't belong here."

When the baker heard the meaning of the butler's dream, he was hopeful. So he said, "In my dream I saw myself walking along with three baskets of baked goods on my head, but the birds came and ate everything in the top basket."

"The three baskets are three days," Joseph told him. "In three days Pharaoh will order you to be hanged, and vultures will eat your body."

Three days later it was Pharaoh's birthday, and things happened just as Joseph had said. But when the butler got his job back, he forgot all about Joseph (Gen. 40).

Pharaoh

Two years went by, and one night Pharaoh had two dreams that really disturbed him. In the first he saw seven fat cows come out of a river, followed by seven lean cows. Then the seven lean cows ate the seven fat ones. Pharaoh woke up, troubled about such a strange dream.

Finally he fell back asleep and dreamed of seven fat ears of corn that sprang out of one cornstalk, followed by seven thin ones blighted by the east wind. Then the seven thin ears of corn ate the seven fat ones. Again Pharaoh woke up, and this time what he had seen especially bothered him.

In the morning he called in his counselors and wise men and told them his dreams, but no one could tell him what they meant. That's when the butler remembered Joseph. He told Pharaoh what had happened in prison and that a Hebrew slave had interpreted his dream.

Immediately Pharaoh sent for him. Quickly Joseph shaved, changed his prison clothes, and followed the guards to the palace. When he arrived, Pharaoh asked him if he could interpret dreams.

"Your Majesty, I don't interpret dreams, but God does. He will let us know what they mean." So Pharaoh told Joseph the two dreams.

"Your Majesty, the two dreams are one," Joseph said. "They were given to you twice to emphasize the certainty of what will happen. The seven fat cows and seven fat ears of corn represent seven years of plenty. The seven lean cows and seven thin ears of corn depict seven years of famine. Pharaoh needs to store up food during the seven good years so the people will have enough to eat during the seven bad years, and he needs to appoint a special officer to see that this gets done" (Gen. 41:1-36).

Joseph's Rise to Power

The interpretation made sense to Pharaoh and his officials. So Pharaoh asked, "Where else can we find a man like this who has God's Spirit in him?" Then he turned to Joseph and said, "Because God told you the meaning of my dreams, I'm appointing you as governor of Egypt to see that this gets done."

He handed Joseph his ring, had his servants put a royal robe on him, and hung a gold chain around his neck. Then he changed Joseph's name to Zaphenath Paneah and gave him the daughter of the high priest for a wife. Providing Joseph with horses and a chariot, the king had him ride behind him throughout the city. The royal guards went ahead of them and told the people to bow to Pharaoh and to Joseph, the governor.

Joseph was 30 years old when this happened (Gen. 41:37-46).

Prosperity and Famine

So Joseph took charge, and for the next seven years, when the harvests produced much more than usual, he stored all the grain he could.

During this time he had two sons. The first one he named Manasseh, meaning "God has helped me forget." The second son he named Ephraim, "God has blessed me."

Then came the seven years of famine, just as God had said they would. The famine even spread to nearby countries. When people needed grain and came to Pharaoh for help, he sent them to Joseph, who opened the storehouses and sold grain to Egyptians and foreigners alike (Gen. 41:47-57).

Joseph's Brothers

When Jacob heard that Egypt still had grain, he told his sons to stop complaining about the famine and buy what they needed in Egypt. All the sons went, except Benjamin, because Jacob refused to let him go.

When they got to Egypt, the officials directed them to the governor in charge of the grain supplies. Joseph immediately knew his brothers, but they didn't recognize him, and when they bowed to him, his mind went back to the dreams he'd had years before.

Through an interpreter he asked, "Where are you men from?"

"From Canaan," they answered.

So he accused them of having come to spy out the land and discover the weak points in Egypt's defenses.

"No, my lord!" they protested. "We are all brothers, 12 sons of one man. One is dead and the youngest one is at home. We've come only to buy grain to feed our families."

"How can I know that you're telling me the truth?" Joseph demanded. "There's one way to find out. I want one of you to go back to get your younger brother—you decide which one should go—while the rest of you stay here. Until then I'm putting you under arrest."

Three days later Joseph had them brought back to see him and said, "In the fear of God, I have thought about this and have changed my mind. I've decided to have only one of you stay. The rest of you may return home."

They talked among themselves and concluded, "All this is happening to us because of the way we treated Joseph."

"Didn't I tell you not to do that?" Reuben said. "But you wouldn't listen!"

Joseph understood everything they said, but they didn't know it and kept arguing. It got to be too much for him, so he left the room and wept. When he returned they still hadn't decided, so he chose Simeon as the one to stay. Joseph ordered Simeon's hands tied and had him led away as his brothers watched (Gen. 42:1-24).

Money Problems

Then Joseph gave them permission to buy grain and told his steward to hide their money in the sacks. So the brothers loaded their donkeys and headed for home. On the way one of them opened his sack to feed his donkey and found his money bag inside. Shocked, he called out to his brothers, "Come! Look! My money bag is in my sack on top of the grain!" He pulled it out and showed it to them, and they didn't know what to think.

When they arrived at home, they told Jacob everything that had happened and that Simeon would be in prison until they returned with Benjamin. Then they emptied their sacks, and each man found his money bag. That really scared them. How could they explain to the governor that they had paid for the grain when they still had the money?

Shocked, Jacob said, "Simeon is in prison, and you think I should let Benjamin go to Egypt next time? Oh, no!"

"Put Benjamin in my care, Father," Reuben announced, "and I'll bring him back. I promise on the life of my own two sons!"

But their father would not change his mind. "Do you want to kill me? If anything happens to Benjamin, I'll die" (Gen. 42:25–38).

Benjamin

The famine continued, and when they had eaten all their grain, Jacob asked his sons to go back to Egypt to get some more. "The governor explicitly warned us not to come back without Benjamin!" Judah reminded him. "We can't go there without him!"

"Why did you do this to me?" Jacob demanded.

"The governor asked us if we had other brothers," they tried to explain. "So we told him that one was dead and the youngest one was at home. How could we know that this would happen?"

"Please, Father, let Benjamin go with us!" Judah pleaded. "If we don't get more grain, we'll all die! I'm willing to take the blame if anything happens to him."

Finally Jacob relented and said, "All right, take some spices and honey and almonds with you as gifts for the governor, and double the money to pay for the new grain and for what you got last time. Take Benjamin, and may God help the governor to be merciful. If I have to lose Simeon and Benjamin, I don't know how I will bear the pain! But what else can I do?"

So the brothers left for Egypt, and when Joseph saw them, he said to his steward, "Take those men to my house and have the cook prepare a meal for all of us."

When told that they would eat with the governor, Joseph's brothers got scared and said among themselves, "He's going to accuse us of stealing the money we found in our sacks and make us his slaves!"

They talked to the steward and told him they had brought back the money to pay for the grain they had bought before and that they had no idea how it got there.

"Don't be afraid," he assured them. "I put the money back in your sacks. It's a gift from the God of your father." Then he brought Simeon out and took them all to Joseph's house. When they arrived, the steward provided food for their donkeys and asked them to get ready to eat with the governor.

When Joseph arrived at noon, the brothers bowed and gave him the presents they had brought along. He thanked them and then asked, "How is your father, the old man you told me about? Is he well?"

They bowed and told him that he was doing as well as could be expected for his age. Then Joseph looked at Benjamin and asked, "Is this your younger brother? God be gracious to you, my son."

It was all too much for Joseph. Overcome with emotion, he excused himself and went to his bedroom and cried. Then he washed his face, came back out, and asked that everyone be served. Joseph sat by himself and so did his servants, because custom would not allow Egyptians to eat at the same table with people from Canaan.

The brothers were amazed that they had been seated according to age and wondered how the steward could have known that. As they were being served, Benjamin received more food than they did. But they weren't jealous. Instead, they were happy for him and enjoyed being together (Gen. 43:11-34).

The Silver Cup

After the meal, Joseph told his steward to see to it that the sacks of the men were filled with grain, to put each man's money back in his sack, and to place Joseph's own silver cup in Benjamin's sack. The next morning the brothers left for home.

They had barely gotten out of the city when Joseph sent his steward after them. When the servant caught up with them, he said, "Why are you men so wicked after we have been so good to you? Why did you steal the governor's silver cup?"

Stunned, the brothers replied, "Sir, we wouldn't do such a thing! If you find the silver cup in someone's sack, let that man die, and we'll all go back and be the governor's slaves!"

"Only the one who stole the cup will become a slave," the steward told them. "The rest of you are free to go."

Each man opened his sack, and the steward looked into each one, beginning with the sack of the oldest brother. When he dug into Benjamin's sack, he found the cup.

The brothers couldn't believe it! Tearing their robes, they loaded their donkeys and headed back into the city to see the governor. There they fell on their knees. Joseph looked sternly at them and said, "Don't you realize that I have ways of finding things out? Why did you do this?"

"My lord, what can we say?" Judah managed to say. "We don't know how the cup got there. But we are willing to be your slaves to remain with the one in whose sack the cup was found. Do to us as you wish."

"Your brother will be my slave. The rest of you can return home."

Judah then stepped forward again and said, "My lord, please listen to me! We know you have the power of Pharaoh. Last year you asked about our father and if we had any other brothers. We told you about our family, and you requested that we bring our younger brother next time. When we needed grain again, our father told us to buy some more. Although we told him that we couldn't go back unless our young brother came with us, our old father refused. He said, 'This boy is the love of my life. If I lose him, too, I'll die.' I promised our father that I would bring our young brother back if it cost me my own life. Please, let me take his place and be your slave, and let Benjamin return home. I couldn't stand even to think of what it would do to our father to lose his youngest son."

That was too much for Joseph. After ordering everyone else out of the room, he broke down in tears in front of his brothers. He sobbed so loud that his servants heard it and told Pharaoh. His brothers were shocked to see the governor crying in front of them and didn't know what to think. When Joseph gained control of himself, he said to his brothers in Hebrew, "I'm Joseph, your brother! My father, is he well?"

His brothers stood there stunned! They couldn't believe their ears. "Come close to me," Joseph urged. "I am your brother. God has let this happen for a reason. There have been two years of famine, and there are five more years to come. Hurry home and tell Father that his son Joseph is still alive, and bring him and your families to Egypt. I'll take care of all of you." Then he hugged Benjamin and kissed him on both cheeks, as well as all his brothers.

Pharaoh heard what had happened and was happy for Joseph. Summoning him, the king said, "Tell your brothers to take as much grain as they can put on their animals, and give them wagons to bring your father and their families back here to live. I'll give them the best of Egypt."

Joseph thanked Pharaoh and did what he said. He provided his brothers with wagons, food for their trip, and each with a change of clothes, but he gave Benjamin several changes of clothes and 300 pieces of silver. Also, he sent with them 20 male and female donkeys, loaded with grain and many other good things from Egypt. Then he told them not to argue along the way.

When they reached home and told their father that Joseph was alive and that he was the governor of Egypt, Jacob's heart skipped a beat or two. He couldn't believe it! But when he saw the wagons and the loaded donkeys, he got excited and said, "Joseph is alive! I must go and see him!" (Gen. 44:1-45:28).

Jacob Goes to Egypt

Then Jacob offered sacrifices of thanksgiving to the Lord and prepared to leave for Egypt. That night God called to him: "Jacob!"

"Here I am!"

"Don't be afraid—I'll go with you to Egypt. You will see Joseph, and he will take care of you."

The brothers put their father and the women and children in the wagons Pharaoh had given them, and they also took their flocks and herds along. Sixty-six descendants of Jacob went to Egypt, not counting Joseph and his family, who were already there, making a total of 70.

As they approached Egypt, Jacob sent Judah ahead to tell Joseph they were coming. Overjoyed, Joseph quickly asked for his chariot and went to meet them. When he saw his father, he drove up, jumped out of the chariot, and ran to him. They hugged each other and cried for a long time. Then Jacob said, "Now I can die in peace, because I have seen my son and know that he's alive and well."

When they got to Egypt, Joseph said to his brothers, "Let me go tell Pharaoh that you're here and that you've brought your flocks and herds with you. When he calls you in and asks what you do for a living, say to him that you've taken care of flocks and herds all your lives. Egyptians don't like shepherds, but Pharaoh will welcome you and let you settle in the area of Goshen, away from the Egyptians."

Joseph decided to take five of his brothers to see Pharaoh, introduced them, and said, "Your Majesty, these are five of my brothers who have come to live here."

Pharaoh greeted them and asked, "What do you do for a living? What's your occupation?"

"Your Majesty, we are shepherds, just as our ancestors were," the brothers answered. "We have come from Canaan, because the famine there is bad. Please let us settle somewhere where we can take care of our flocks and herds."

Even though they told Pharaoh that they were shepherds, he turned to Joseph and said, "Goshen is a good choice, since it's one of the more fertile places in Egypt. Let them settle there."

Then Joseph went to get his father to meet Pharaoh. When Jacob came in, he bowed before Pharaoh, then raised his hand and blessed him. Pharaoh thanked Jacob, looked at him, and asked, "How old are you?"

"I'm 130 years old. My ancestors lived a lot longer, but I've had a hard life." They talked awhile, and before Jacob left, he blessed Pharaoh again.

Then Joseph helped his father and brothers and their families settle in Goshen and provided enough food for all of them (Gen. 46:1-47:12).

The Famine Continues

The famine became so severe that it began to affect even the people in Egypt. Joseph had put all the money he collected from selling grain into Pharaoh's treasury. When the people ran out of money, they used their animals to pay for grain, and when they no longer had animals, they offered Joseph their fields. He agreed and gave them grain, with the understanding that one fifth of the crops from then on would go to Pharaoh. The people accepted his proposal, thanked Joseph for saving their lives, and worked the fields that now belonged to Pharaoh.

However, Pharaoh had made a different arrangement with the priests: he gave them the grain they needed so they could keep their animals and their land (Gen. 47:13-26).

Jacob's Last Days

Seventeen years had passed since Jacob had come to Egypt with his sons and had settled in Goshen. He was 147 years old, extremely weak, and realized that it wouldn't be long before he would die. So he sent for Joseph and said to him, "I want you to take a vow and promise me that you will not bury me in Egypt, but will take my body back to Canaan and bury me next to Abraham and Isaac." Joseph took an oath and promised he would honor his father's wishes.

Not long afterward, word came to Joseph that his father was terribly sick and that he would probably die any day. So Joseph took his two sons, Manasseh and Ephraim, and rushed to Goshen to see his father. When Joseph entered, Jacob forced himself to sit up in bed and said, "Years ago God told me that Canaan would be ours and that our family would become a great people. That includes your two sons."

Because Jacob was almost blind, he had to ask Joseph, "Are these two young men your boys? Bring them close so I can put my hands on them and bless them." Joseph brought them close, with Manasseh on his right and Ephraim on his left. Jacob hugged the boys, kissed them on both cheeks, and put his right hand on Ephraim and his left on Manasseh.

"Father! Wait! Manasseh is the firstborn!" Joseph said. "You should put your right hand on him!"

When he tried to switch his father's hands, Jacob resisted and said, "I know, my son, but Ephraim will become stronger and greater than Manasseh."

Keeping his hands the way he had them, Jacob said, "May the God of Abraham bless these two young men. Let them be like my own sons, sons of Israel, and may they have many descendants."

Then he looked at Joseph and said, "I know I'm dying, but God will be with you and will take you and your brothers back to Canaan. I want you and your sons to have the fertile area of Shechem, which I got from the Amorites" (Gen. 47:27-48:22).

A Father's Blessing

Jacob was ready to bless all his sons, so he asked them to gather around his bed. "Listen to your old father!" he began. "Let me tell you what shall come to pass.

"Reuben, you are my firstborn. You're dignified and strong, but you're also unstable, like the time you embarrassed me by sleeping with Rachel's maid. Simeon and Levi, both of you are very strong but can also be very cruel. Judah, your brothers will praise you for your unselfishness. You're like a lion, and kings will come from your descendants, including Shiloh, the Promised One.

"Zebulun, you love the sea, and your descendants will serve as sea traders. Issachar, you're as strong as a donkey, and you love the land and will work it well. Dan, you are as wise as a serpent, and your descendants will be rulers and judges. Gad, your people are fighters, and even when you're defeated, you will come back and win. Asher, your descendants will provide food and delicacies fit for royalty. Naphtali, you're like a deer who loves freedom. You're good with words, and your descendants will be also.

"Joseph, you're steady and true. Your arms are made strong by the Mighty One, the Shepherd and Protector of Israel. You're like a deep stream, and through your two sons you will have a double portion in Israel. And Benjamin, you have the disposition of a wolf that doesn't give up but gets what it goes after."

When he had finished blessing his sons, Jacob said, "I'm about to die. Be sure to take my body back home and bury me in the cave with Abraham and Sarah, Isaac and Rebekah, and where I buried Leah." Then he lay back down and died (Gen. 49).

Jacob's Burial

Joseph cried, fell on his father's face, and kissed him. Then he called for the physicians to embalm the body, which took 40 days, the normal time for embalming, and the Egyptians mourned for Joseph's father for an additional 30 days.

When the time of mourning was over, Joseph went to see Pharaoh's officials and said, "Kindly tell Pharaoh for me about the promise I made to my father to take his body back to Canaan and bury him next to his ancestors. Ask him to please allow me to go—I will come back."

They went to see Pharaoh to ask him to let Joseph leave to bury his father in Canaan. "Joseph has my permission," the Egyptian ruler said.

So Joseph and his brothers and their families left to bury Jacob, and Pharaoh's officials, the leading men of Egypt, and all of Joseph's servants went with them. The only Israelites left behind were the children and those taking care of the flocks and herds.

When the Canaanites saw all the horses and wagons, they said to one another, "This must have been a very important person for so many Egyptians to mourn this way." Then Jacob's sons placed their father in the cave next to Abraham and Isaac, as he had requested, and they all returned to Egypt (Gen. 50:1-14).

Joseph's Brothers

When they arrived back home, the brothers said to each other, "Now that our father is dead, Joseph will get even with us." So they sent word to him reminding him that their father had asked him to forgive them, and pleaded with him to do so.

Joseph cried when he received their message and asked to see them. The brothers came, bowed to him, and offered to be his slaves. Joseph said, "I'm not God! What you did to me was wrong, but God turned it into something good. So don't worry—I've forgiven you, and I'll do all I can for you and your families." He spoke kindly to them, and they believed what he said and took it to heart (Gen. 50:15-21).

Joseph Dies

Joseph lived to see his grandchildren and great-grandchildren. When he was about to die, he called for his family and said, "Promise me that when you go back home, you'll take my body with you and bury me in Canaan."

They took an oath and promised they would bury him there. A short time later Joseph died, and the Egyptians embalmed him and placed his body in a coffin. He was 110 years old (Gen. 50:22-26).

five

Job

During the time of the patriarchs (Abraham, Isaac, and Jacob) a man named Job lived in the land of Uz, east of Canaan.

A good man who loved God and hated evil, he had 10 children (seven sons and three daughters), and he owned thousands of sheep and camels, plus hundreds of donkeys. Lots of people worked for him, and he was the richest man in that part of the country.

His sons would take turns hosting family get-togethers, and after such banquets, Job would get up early the next morning to offer a sacrifice for each of his children. He would say to himself, "Maybe they said or did something to displease God without realizing it" (Job 1:1-5).

God and Satan

Now, there came a day in heaven when God called a meeting of His representatives throughout the universe. Satan showed up and wanted to be allowed in. The Lord asked him, "What right do you have to attend?" Satan answered, "I represent Planet Earth."

God said, "Have you noticed my servant Job? He is a good man who respects Me and hates everything evil."

"Do You think he's doing it for nothing?" Satan snapped back. "You're always protecting him and blessing him. If he loses what he has, he'll turn against You and curse You."

God responded, "Let's see who is right, then. Everything he possesses is in your hands, but don't touch him personally."

In one day Satan destroyed everything that Job had. A messenger came running to Job and said, "Raiders killed your servants who were plowing the fields, and they also seized all your oxen and donkeys!" No sooner had the first messenger finished speaking than another messenger arrived, who said, "Sir, a storm came up, and lightning struck and killed all your shepherds and sheep!" Then a third messenger gasped, "Sir, horsemen came out of nowhere, killed your herdsmen, and rode off with all your camels!" Immediately a fourth messenger followed, saying, "O sir, while your sons and daughters were eating at your oldest son's house, a tornado came out of nowhere and hit the house, and they've all been killed!"

Job couldn't believe it! Rising to his feet, he tore his robe, shaved his head, then threw himself to the ground, crying, "I came into this world with nothing, and I will leave with nothing! The Lord gives, and the Lord takes away. Blessed be the name of the Lord!" Through all this tragedy, Job did not blame God (Job 1).

Satan wanted to attend the next meeting God had with His representatives from the universe. "I see you're back," the Lord said to him. "What do you think of My servant Job? He's still faithful, and he worships Me even though in one day he lost everything he had."

"A man will do anything to be healthy and stay alive," Satan argued. "You take away his health so that he thinks he's going to die, and he'll turn against You and curse You to Your face."

"Let's see who's right," God replied. "You may do what you want to him, but don't take his life."

After Satan left, he made Job break out with festering boils all over his body. Shocked at what had happened to him, Job took off his robe and went to the city's garbage dump, where he sat down and scraped off the pus that oozed from his sores. Then his wife came and said to him, "Why don't you just curse God and die!"

Looking at her with pity, Job said, "You're very foolish to talk that way. When God did good things for us, you thanked Him and praised His name. When He lets something bad happen, you want me to curse Him."

As sick and as miserable as Job was, he did not turn against God (Job 2:1-10).

Job's Three Friends

When three of Job's friends heard what had happened, they came looking for him. But when they saw him, they could hardly recognize him. They were so shocked that they tore their robes in grief, sprinkled dust on their heads, and sat down near him and cried. Then they stayed there for an entire week, not saying a word, grieving with their friend.

Finally Job spoke up. "May the day perish on which I was born! Why didn't I die at birth? If I had, I would sleep and be at rest. Why did I have to live! I groan in pain, and I don't want to eat. What I dreaded has happened to me. I have lost my health and have no peace or rest" (Job 2:11-3:26).

Friend Number 1

"Job, I just can't keep quiet any longer," Eliphaz began. "Listen to me and don't get upset with what I'm going to say. You've helped and encouraged a lot of people when they were sick. Now it's your turn to be sick, and you can't take it.

"Stop and think. Do terrible things like this happen to good people? It's when they are bad that God punishes them. Some never understand this, and when they're dying, they still wonder why things happened to them the way they did.

"Trouble doesn't come from nowhere. People bring it on themselves. What you need to do is turn back to God. He loves those who are humble, and He will forgive you.

"Accept the fact that God is correcting you, confess your sins, and He will bind up your wounds and make you well again. Then you can go back to your house healthy and strong, live to a ripe old age, and have many descendants" (Job 4:1–5:27).

Job Responds

"Oh, that people could feel my pain and know how much I'm suffering! God, are You against me? This is more than I can take. I wish You would let me die. At least then I would be at rest. Why should I prolong my life? Even animals let us know when they're hungry or in pain.

"Friends should be kind to a friend when he is suffering, even if they think he has turned against God. Did I ever disappoint any of you? Did I ever take advantage of your friendship or ask you for help? If so, tell me what I did wrong. Be honest with me. Have I ever been unjust to anyone?

"Hard times come to everyone, and now they have struck me. I haven't had a good night's sleep for months. I keep tossing and turning, wondering why the nights are so long. During the night my skin keeps cracking, pus oozes from my boils, and when I get up in the morning, I'm covered with maggots.

"My days are without hope. Will I ever live to see good times again? Will people welcome me back and be glad to see me? In one sense, all of us are like clouds that come and go. We die and are gone, never to return home and see our loved ones again.

"But while I'm still alive, I will speak up. Do you three have to just sit there and stare at me as if I'm a poisonous snake you have to keep your eyes on? I hate the way I am, and I don't want to live.

"Lord, what are human beings, anyway? Why would You set Your heart on them and attend to all their needs? And why do You keep watching me? What have I done? If I have sinned against You, can't You forgive me? Oh well, it won't be long before I'll be gone" (Job 6:1-7:21).

Friend Number 2

"Job, your words are as empty as the wind," Bildad protested. "Is God ever unfair? He let your sons and daughters perish from the tornado because they had sinned.

"You need to turn back to God before even more bad things happen to you. If you were pure and upright, He would come to your rescue and prosper you again. Just think what our forefathers had to go through and the lessons they had to learn. Our lives are so short compared to theirs, and our experience is so limited. If they could talk, they would tell you what's right.

"This much we know: grass can't grow without water. As soon as it's cut, it dies. That's what happens to those who ignore God. There's no hope for hypocrites. While God does not abandon the blameless, neither will He bless the wicked.

"Turn back to God, and He will heal you. You will laugh again and shout for joy, and those who hate you will be put to shame" (Job 8:1-22).

Job Answers

"I know that God blesses the righteous," Job said. "But how can a man be righteous before God? Is he going to argue his way out of what he did?

"God knows everything, and His power is awesome. He moves mountains and shakes the whole earth. The sun and the stars listen to Him, and the constellations obey Him. Who's going to stop Him and ask, 'What are You doing?' Even if I were righteous, how could I plead my case with Him? He knows so much more about me than I do about myself.

"No matter what I do, if I went and took a bath, changed my clothes, and put on a smile, you would still say that God brought all these things on me because I had sinned.

"Since God is not a human being, we can't go to court to settle the issue. Who would be the judge and mediate between us and our differences? Just thinking about His power overwhelms me! If He would turn His might away from me, I wouldn't be so afraid of speaking up.

"God, please don't condemn me. Tell me why all this has happened to me. You created me, and Your hands fashioned me. Why would You turn against me? You gave me life, and I know that You care for my soul. When I sin, You know it and don't overlook it, and when I'm good, I have nothing to be proud of.

"Why did You let me be born? Please don't bother with me, and let me have a little peace and comfort before I die and go to the place of no return" (Job 9:1-10:22).

Friend Number 3

"Someone has to answer Job in a way that will make him listen," Zophar insisted. "We can't support what he says, because he keeps justifying his actions.

"Job, you think you have things right and that in your own eyes you're good. If God spoke to you, however, you'd be more careful about what you say.

"Do you think you can understand Him? He knows the heart of everyone and will not overlook sin. The problem is that human beings are so stubborn that they won't listen, and that applies to you.

"You need to turn back to God, confess your sins, and put your wickedness behind you. Then He will lift you up, your health will return, and your fears will be gone. Your life will shine as the noonday sun, you will be full of hope, and you will sleep at night without worry. In the morning people will again come to you for favors.

"But sinners are without hope and will not escape their final end" (Job 11).

Job Replies

"You three speak as if you have all the answers. But I'm just as intelligent as you are and know a few things too. I thought you were my friends! Yet you talk to me as if I never knew God and never received any answers to prayer.

"Look at the animals. Their lives are in God's hand and so are ours. The Lord knows what He's doing. He tears down and builds up. He makes fools out of judges and overthrows the mighty. He uncovers the darkness and brings out the light. He makes nations great and then brings them to an end. Their leaders grope in darkness and stagger like drunkards. I've seen it with my own eyes.

"But I'd rather talk about God. Sure, you come up with all kinds of ideas about me, yet you're like worthless physicians. How can you presume to speak for the Lord about me? How will you fare when He examines *you?*

"Let me speak! Even if God decided to kill me, I would still love Him. He is my salvation. Listen to me! When He takes up my case, I'll be vindicated.

"O God, don't withdraw from me, and don't let me be afraid of You. Please listen to me, and let me know what I have done wrong. Why did

You bring all these things on me as if I'm Your enemy? Look at me! I'm nothing but a dry leaf blown by the wind, like a rotting piece of wood.

"A person's life is brief and full of problems. You are the one who decides how long they should live. Humanity is like a flower that blooms one day and is gone the next. There's more hope for a tree! After it's cut down, the roots sense water, and the tree sprouts again. But when a human being dies, they're gone. Will they live again? Once I die, I'll have to wait in the grave until You call, and when You do, I will answer. I will rise from the grave, my sins will be gone, and my record will be clean. Meanwhile, death is a painful reality, and the human spirit mourns" (Job 12:1-14:22).

Friend Number 1

Then Eliphaz took up the discussion again: "Is a wise person unreasonable? Do they say things that don't make sense? Job, you claim to be wise, but from what you're saying, you're condemning yourself.

"What do you know that we don't? We have listened to men older than your father. As your friends, we have been gentle with you, but you just sit there and glare at us. When you don't listen, you're turning more and more away from God.

"Can a person ever be so innocent and pure that they can claim to be sinless? Even angels don't speak of themselves as being holy before God. How much less holy are men who drink in evil like water!

"Listen to me! Wicked individuals face no end of troubles and are always afraid that they'll lose what they have. They fight with God as if He were their enemy. Wealth will not last forever, so we ought not to deceive ourselves by putting our trust in what we have" (Job 15).

Job Responds

"You are miserable comforters!" Job groaned. "Don't you ever run out of things to say? If our roles were reversed, I could sit there and say the same things about you, but I wouldn't think of doing that. I would comfort you and try to relieve you of your suffering and grief.

"Even if I kept quiet as you want me to, my pain and grief wouldn't stop. You have worn me out and have only made things worse for me. I feel as if God has turned me over to my enemies and taken me by the neck and given me a good shaking, even though I haven't wronged anyone. I can't stop crying.

"I do have a Friend in heaven who stands up for me, no matter what my friends down here say about me. He will plead my case.

"It won't be long now. I'm having a hard time breathing. I'm losing my eyesight. My arms and legs are as thin as rails. I feel as if my friends have come to spit in my face. Not one of them understands what I'm going through, nor can they change my night into day.

"The grave is my only hope of relief. Death will be my father, and worms, my mother and sister. But how long can hope alone sustain me?" (Job 16:1-17:16).

Friend Number 2

"Job, when will you stop talking and listen?" Bildad demanded. "Do you think we're stupid? Why do you get so upset when we're trying to tell you something?

"You know what happens to those who are wicked. They get caught in their own net. Trapped, they can't get out. They try to stand on their own feet but are not able to, and as they struggle, they lose more and more strength. The light of their life grows dim, and terror grips their heart.

"Disease ravishes their bodies. Like a dying tree, their leaves shrivel, their branches become empty, and their roots dry up. Soon they are gone and no one remembers them. That's what happens to the wicked, to those who turn away from God" (Job 18).

Job Answers

"How much longer are you going to torment me?" Job exploded. "Why do you keep hammering me to pieces with your words? Why are you so against me?

"No matter what you say, I still feel that God has wronged me. I cry out to Him in pain, but He does not hear me. What is happening to me is not fair. He has taken away my wealth, destroyed my reputation, and robbed me of my dignity. Viewing me as His enemy, He has broken me down until my hope is gone.

"My brothers don't come to see me, my relatives ignore me, and my friends have forgotten me. When I call for one of my servants, he acts as if he doesn't hear me. My wife can't stand to come near me, and my grandchildren don't care to see me. Even you, my closest friends, have turned against me.

"I'm nothing but skin and bones. The least you can do is to have pity on me. God has abandoned me, and now so have you. I wish my words could be written down and engraved in stone so that others could read them.

"But one thing I know: my Redeemer lives, and one day He'll come to earth. And even if I die and my skin is gone, I will see Him—not through someone else's eyes but with my own! Oh, how I long for that day!

"You say that the root of my troubles is in me. Be careful what you say, because all of us have to face the judgment someday. The sword of the Lord is against evil. You know that" (Job 19).

Friend Number 3

"Job, what you say upsets me," Zophar protested. "Why do you keep it up? Don't you know that the triumph of the wicked is short and the joy of the hypocrite doesn't last? A wicked person may seem great, but eventually they'll disappear like a bad dream. Their children try to make things right by giving back to the poor what their fathers took from them, but it's too late.

"Evil is sweet to the mouth of the wicked, but when they swallow it, it's like taking poison into their stomachs, and they vomit up their wealth. Their greed is never satisfied, the profits of their businesses offer no lasting joy, and they have no peace of mind. God will expose their sins and punish them for what they have done, and everything they once had will be gone. That is the fate of the wicked" (Job 20).

Job Replies

"All I ask is that you listen to what I have to say," Job begged. "Bear with me, and when I'm done, you can laugh if you wish.

"My complaint is not against what people think of me, but against God. Look at me! Doesn't it shock you? When I think of all that has happened to me, I begin shaking all over and am afraid of what else will happen to me.

"Why does God let the wicked live so long? They live to see their children grow up and rejoice with their grandchildren. Or why does God let evil people become so powerful? Disaster never strikes them, they spend their days in wealth, their houses are safe, their herds and flocks continue to increase, and their children run and play without fear. They turn their backs on God, never feel the need to pray, and then die without suffering. When does God punish them for their wickedness?

"Life isn't fair. One person lives at ease, is healthy and strong, and then dies. Another struggles in poverty and dies with a heart full of bitterness. The rich have a tomb, and many attend their funeral to pay their respects, but no one comes to honor a homeless person, and they get buried in unmarked graves. The worms don't care—they'll eat all of them, rich and poor alike.

"So why do you try to comfort me with dumb arguments about tragedy afflicting only the wicked? What you're saying doesn't make sense" (Job 21).

Friend Number 1

For a third time Eliphaz responded: "Job, what benefit is it to God if you're righteous? He doesn't punish people for nothing.

"All these things have happened to you because you have sinned. Most likely you have forced people to pay what they owed you even if it left them naked. Maybe you were not concerned about the homeless as you should have been and did nothing to feed the hungry. What did you do for the widows and orphans?

"God knows all this. You can't hide it from Him. The possessions of the wicked suddenly get swept away by floods, and their vineyards dry up from the heat. All this happens to them, but they still don't turn to God, even though He gave them all they had to begin with.

"Turn back to God and listen to what He says! You'll be at peace, and He'll give you back everything you had before, including silver and gold. He'll answer your prayers and brighten your days, and once again your life will be full of hope" (Job 22).

Job Responds

"Oh, I wish I knew where to find the Lord!" Job sighed. "I would go to Him and present my case. I know He would listen to me and declare me innocent.

"In my mind I'm looking everywhere for Him but can't find Him. Yet I know He's here. He knows where I am, and after He's tested me, my life will come out as gold. I have walked in His way and have not turned aside. I have kept His commandments and have treasured His words.

"What God wants to do, He does, and no one can stop Him. That's why I'm afraid of what else He might do to me. He could have taken my life, but so far He hasn't.

"God knows everything. Some people move boundary lines, and others steal from a man's flock or take a widow's only cow. They push the needy off the road and force the poor to hide or to run to the mountains for safety. Still others don't hesitate to take a child away from its mother and cause the poor to go hungry. Yet God does nothing to stop it.

"Then there are those who do their evil deeds at night. They kill the innocent, commit adultery, and break into houses, and no one seems to stop them. It would be better if people such as that had never been born. The world would be better off if they would melt away like snow on a hot day.

"God could use His power to stop them but He doesn't. This gives them a sense of false security, and they keep on committing murder, adultery, and breaking into people's houses. It doesn't occur to them that God knows everything they do. They succeed for a while, but suddenly they are taken out of the way.

"Can anyone prove me wrong?" (Job 23:1–24:25).

Friend Number 2

Then Bildad spoke up for the third time and said, "God is awesome and powerful. We all have to stand before Him. But how can a human claim to be righteous in the presence of a holy God?

"Even the sun, moon, and stars are not bright compared to the presence of God. So what about humanity? Compared to God, we're nothing more than a small insect" (Job 25).

Job Replies

"You three are sure a big help to someone who is suffering and who, according to you, doesn't know very much!" Job retorted. "If you think so little of me, why do you bother? What kind of spirit is coming out of your mouth? What are you saying about God and me?

"God is so powerful that He can do whatever He wants. When He speaks to the grave, the dead hear His voice. He hangs the world on nothing. The Lord transports water in clouds, draws a line where the oceans have to stop, and breaks up storms, no matter how powerful they are. By His Spirit He beautifies the earth and the heavens. All these things are only whispers of His power.

"God has not been fair with me. He has made my life miserable. But as long as I have breath, I will not lie. As long as I live, I will be honest and hold to integrity. I will not put on a front but will tell you the truth and not be hypocritical.

"There's no hope for hypocrites, no matter how rich they are. Do they delight themselves in the Lord? Will God listen to them and answer their prayers? What good is their wealth to them when they die?

"Let me tell you about God's power. On second thought, I don't need to, because you've seen it yourselves. So why do you keep saying that God's actions depend on what we do?" (Job 26:1–27:12).

Friend Number 3*

Zophar interrupted Job, saying, "God will punish the wicked. They may have many sons, but they'll be killed in war. Those who survive will die from sickness and disease, and their remaining children will go hungry.

"Even if they have hills of silver and gold and mountains of clothes, others will get their wealth, and someone else will wear their clothes.

"The beautiful houses that the wicked build are nothing but spider-webs. An evil person goes to sleep at night, and in the early-morning hours, they die and end up with nothing. A tornado comes, and they try to get away but can't, and suddenly everything is gone. That's what happens to those who are wicked" (Job 27:13-23).

Job Responds

"There is a place where silver and gold are mined and where copper and iron are found," Job said in reply. "People dig a mine shaft and hang from ropes, and the earth gives them its treasures of metal. Like eagles and lions, they go after their prey and find it. They dig channels, dam up rivers, and bring out what was hidden.

"They can do all this, but where can they find wisdom? Where can they go for understanding? The ocean says, 'It's not here!' The earth declares, 'It's not in me!' Humanity can't buy wisdom and understanding with silver and gold. There's no price tag on it. Where does it come from? Who has it? Where can you go to get it?

"God knows where you can find it. He knows everything. He made the natural laws for lightning and rain, and He weighs the wind and measures the oceans. God says to human beings, 'The fear of the Lord is wisdom, and to turn from evil is understanding'" (Job 28).

Job's Closing Arguments

"Oh, how I wish I could turn the clock back and it be like it was before! That's when God was good to me, and His light guided me. And that's when I was healthy and strong and walked through darkness unafraid. My children were around me, and my wife loved me. When I went to the gate of the city, young men made way for me, old men rose in respect, and nobles spoke softly.

"I helped the poor, took care of the fatherless, and made widows' hearts sing for joy. Comforting those in grief, I gave counsel to those who needed guidance.

"But things have changed. Now the young men make fun of me and compose crude songs about me. They spit in my face and then walk away.

"It doesn't matter anymore, because I'm about to die, anyway. My bones ache, and there's no end of pain. I've gotten so thin that my robe hangs on me like a sack. God has pushed my face in the mud and left me lying there.

"O God, I call on You for help, but You don't answer. Why are You treating me this way? Don't You have any pity at all on a sick man ready to die? I have cried with people who mourn and helped them in their time of trouble. Why can't You do the same for me?

"My head is in a whirl. I looked forward to a long and happy life, but all I have is pain. I'm burning up with fever, and my skin is cracking and peeling off. Although I plead for help, no one listens. My voice is like the howl of a solitary wolf.

"Years ago I made an agreement with myself to watch my behavior and never to look at a young woman to lust after her. I told myself that I would do nothing to displease God.

"I have not lied or acted wickedly. Never have I mistreated anyone. When my servants had a complaint, I listened to them and treated them fairly, men and women alike. If I had done otherwise, how could I ever face God? He gave me life, just as He did others. I have no more rights than anyone else.

"I never refused to help anyone. If they were poor, I fed them, or if they needed clothing, I gave it to them. Nor did I ignore the orphans and widows. If I'm lying, may my right arm drop off my body!

"I never trusted in silver and gold, nor did I ever feel important because I was rich. I never rejoiced when my enemies suffered or when disasters struck them, and I never cursed anyone. Instead, I have always welcomed strangers passing through and invited them to stay overnight. And I never worried about what people thought of me.

"How I wish that at least one person would believe what I say! Were everything I have done written in a book, I would want it to be open for everyone to read. If I had to, I would not hesitate to stand before God, because I have not done anything to be ashamed of.

"If I'm lying, may my fields grow nothing but thistles and weeds" (Job 29:1–31:40).

Another Friend

Job's three friends stopped arguing with him because he refused to admit having done anything bad enough for God to punish him as severely as apparently He had done.

Then Elihu, one of Job's younger friends, spoke up. Although Job's attempt to justify himself and blame God for being unfair disturbed him, Elihu was really upset with his older friends because all they had done was condemn Job. They never really answered the question of why he was suffering. Now that his three friends had stopped talking, he felt he could say something.

"Job, I'm much younger than you and our other three friends," he began. "That's why I hesitated to say anything. God not only gives wisdom to men of experience, but also to younger ones. I want all of you to listen to me.

"I've been paying close attention to what everyone had to say. But I can't keep quiet any longer. I'm not going to flatter anyone but will talk straight, or God will punish me for sure.

"Job, listen to me! As truly as God has given me life and breath, I will be honest with you. You claim that you're innocent of any wrongdoing, and you think that God is against you. That's your real problem. God does things to save people, not to hurt them. A person may think they're going to die from what's happened, but their Mediator says, 'I have ransomed them—they will not die!' They will be healed and will feel young again and delight themselves in God. That's how the Lord does things. He works again and again with people to bring them back to Himself. Listen to what I say. Don't answer me yet—let me finish."

Then Elihu turned to his three friends and said, "I want you to listen to me too. Job claims to be innocent. He says God is not being fair, and he wonders whether it really pays to serve Him. That's Job's real problem, not his sins! God is never unfair, and He doesn't pervert justice. If He decided to turn away from us, we would all die.

"The Lord isn't partial, and He doesn't treat kings and princes any differently than the rest of us. If He took back the life He gave us, we would all die, whether we're rich or poor. It's the same with nations as it is with individuals. You say that Job lacks wisdom, that he speaks without thinking, and that he doesn't admit that he has sinned. It is not for us to say what Job's sins are. His problem is that he's rebelling against God!

"Job, it's not right for you to claim innocence and charge that God is not fair. Do you think you're more righteous than the Lord is and that you know more than He does? Why would you even hint that it may not pay to serve God?

"Let me say something to you and to our friends. Look at the heavens! See how high they are! What benefit are you to God if you are righteous? Or what can you do to harm Him if you're wicked? The problem is that we don't turn to God for help. We forget that He is our maker, that He's the one who puts a song in our hearts and who gives us wisdom.

"He doesn't answer us because of our pride, because we think we know it all. We're too impatient and feel we need an answer right now! But God's time is not our time, for He knows what is best.

"Now bear with me a little longer! I want to speak on God's behalf. He is no one's enemy, nor does He despise anyone. He is fair with everyone, no matter who they are. He doesn't let the wicked live on and on, nor does He overlook those who are good. Time will reveal His justice. The wicked will perish, and the righteous will be blessed.

"There is no teacher like God. Who will correct Him? Let's not forget

His majesty and power. We see His hand in nature, in the clouds and the rain, in the thunder and the lightning, and in the cycles of light and dark. When I hear thunder, my heart jumps, and when I see lightning streak across the sky, I take notice. I can't explain how God does such things. The Lord tells it to rain or snow and it does, or He commands the lakes to freeze over and they do. He speaks to the animals and directs them to go into their dens because winter is coming, and they obey what He says.

"Job, just stop and think what God can do. It's awesome! He controls the wind, the waves, the sun, and the moon. How should we respond to Him? Should we tell Him what to do? He knows more than we do, and He's never unfair. No wonder He doesn't listen to those who think they know it all" (Job 32:1-37:24).

God Speaks

Then God spoke to Job out of a whirlwind and said, "I want to ask you a question, Job, and I want you to answer me like a man. Where were you when I created this world? Tell me! Did you hear the stars sing and the angels shout for joy?

"What does the earth rest on? Where is its foundation? Who put a limit on the oceans? Did you tell the sun when to come up and when to go down? Do you know where the springs of water in the oceans are? Can you tell me about death? Have you been there and come back? Tell me!

"Do you know all about the east wind, the snow and hail, the thunder, lightning, and rain, and about the trees and grass and why they grow? Do you know about the stars, the constellations, the belt of Orion, the Great Bear and its cubs, and can you tell them where to go? Does the lightning listen to you? Can you control the clouds?

"Do you feed the animals of the world? Can you satisfy the appetites of young lions and nourish the ravens? Do you know when the mountain goats and deer are giving birth? Can you make their young ones grow to be healthy and strong?

"Did you put the free spirit into the wild donkey? Will the wild ox serve you willingly and plow the fields for you? What about the ostrich? Why is it not afraid of riders and horses? Or consider the horse? Where does it get its strength from? It paws the valley and charges into battle, unafraid. Did you give the hawk and eagle sharp eyes and wisdom to know where to fly?

"Are you telling me what I should and shouldn't do? Speak up! Answer Me!"

"Lord, what can I say?" Job answered. "I will put my hand over my mouth and be quiet."

"I'm going to ask you another question," God continued, "and I want an answer! Are you going to clothe yourself in majesty and power and sit in judgment of Me? Can you take care of the wickedness in this world? Are you going to save yourself?

"What about the hippopotamus, especially the big male? Although he eats grass, his legs are like beams of steel and his ribs, like iron. He wades into strong rivers and lets the water flow through his mouth. Nothing seems to bother him.

"What about the mammoth crocodile? Will he let you pull him out of the water with a fishhook? Will he speak softly to you and beg you to let him go? Will he let you play with him as you would a bird? If you decide to lay your hands on him, don't forget the battle you will face! He has rows of scales like plates of armor, and his teeth are as sharp as nails. His eyes look as if they're on fire, and his heart muscle is as hard as a rock. A spear can't touch him, and swords do no good, and when he swims, he leaves a wake behind him. There's no other creature like him."

"Lord," Job replied quietly, "I said things I shouldn't have, and I talked about things I don't really know. You have asked questions I can't answer. I hate myself for saying what I did and ask You to forgive me."

The Lord forgave Job and then said to Eliphaz: "You and your two friends have said things about Me that are not true. Now, I want you to take seven young bulls and seven male sheep and offer them as sacrifices for yourselves, and I will ask Job to pray for each of you."

So that's what Eliphaz, Bildad, and Zophar did—and Job prayed for each of them (Job 38:1-42:9).

God Blesses Job

After this, God not only healed Job and restored what he had lost, but gave him twice as much as he had before. His brothers and sisters and other relatives came to see him and ate with him, and each gave him a piece of silver and a ring of gold. As for his flocks, he soon had twice as many sheep, camels, oxen, and donkeys as he had had previously.

Again Job had seven sons and three daughters. No other women were as beautiful as his three daughters, and he gave them the same inheritance as he did his sons. Job lived for another 140 years and saw his children and grandchildren for four generations. Then he died peacefully at a ripe old age (Job 42:10-17).

---

*Note: Job 27:13-23 is problematic in that the text is contradictory to Job's general position but nevertheless attributed to him in Scripture. Attributing the passage to an interruption by Zophar is an alternate view.

six

Exodus: Coming Out

After Abraham, Isaac, and Jacob had died, and Joseph and his brothers had been laid to rest, a new king came to the throne of Egypt. "There are so many Israelites in the land that if there were a war and they joined forces with our enemies, they could take over the country," he warned his counselors. "Let's put them to work building our cities."

So the king and his officials decided to make the Israelites slaves of the state. But the harder they made them work, the more the Israelites increased in number.

One day the king summoned the Hebrew midwives and said to them, "When you deliver a baby boy, I want you to kill it; but if it's a girl, you can let it live."

The midwives didn't obey the king's order, so he called them back in and asked, "How come you're not doing what I told you to do?"

"The Hebrew women give birth to their babies so quickly that by the time we get there, they're already nursing them," they answered. "We couldn't take those baby boys from their mothers and kill them!" God heard what the midwives said and blessed them for their courage in standing up to the king.

So the king issued an order for the whole country: "All Hebrew baby boys, whether they're nursing or not, are to be killed by throwing them into the river!" (Ex. 1).

Moses

When Baby Moses was born, his parents didn't tell anyone. But when they couldn't keep it a secret any longer, his mother made a little basket, covered it with tar, placed it in the river among the reeds by the shore, and prayed that God would watch over her little one. The baby's sister hid a short distance away to keep an eye on the basket.

That same day the king's daughter came to bathe and to worship, the

Nile being the manifestation of one of their gods, Hapi. As she and her maids walked along the bank, she noticed the basket and asked one of them to get it. When the princess opened the basket and saw the baby, she fell in love with him, held him up, and said, "This is a Hebrew baby! But let's not kill him!"

Moses' sister could hear what the princess said, so she ran up to her and asked, "Would you like me to find a Hebrew woman to nurse it for you?"

The princess answered yes.

So the child ran home and brought her mother back. The princess gave the baby to her and said, "Take him and nurse him for me, and I'll pay you for it."

During his childhood years the princess visited Moses, and when he was 12 years old, she took him to the palace to be educated and trained to be the next king of Egypt. Everyone treated him as the son of the king's daughter. He was educated and trained to be the next king.

One day as Moses was inspecting a construction site, he saw an Egyptian foreman cruelly beating a Hebrew slave. Moses looked around to see if any other Egyptians were nearby, and then he killed the Egyptian foreman and buried him in the sand.

The next day Moses saw two Hebrews fighting with each other. Stopping them, he said to the stronger one, "Don't do that to a fellow Hebrew!"

The man looked at Moses and sneered, "Who made you king? Are you going to kill me, as you did the Egyptian?"

Realizing that his secret was out and that the king would hunt him down and kill him, Moses decided to run for his life. He crossed the border into neighboring Midian, and when he saw a well, he stopped to rest, hoping for a drink of water.

A priest living in the area had seven daughters who would come to the well to water their father's sheep. Other shepherds with their own flocks would push the girls aside. When Moses saw that, he defended the girls and allowed them to take their rightful place in line. That day they got home early and told their father what had happened.

Surprised, he asked, "Where is that Egyptian? Go get him and bring him home to eat with us!"

They did what their father said, and after the meal, Jethro invited Moses to stay with him, which he was glad to do.

As time went on, Moses fell in love with Zipporah, the oldest daughter, and asked her father for permission to marry her. Jethro agreed. When the couple had a son they named him Gershom.

While Moses was in Midian, the king of Egypt died, and the new king was making the Israelites work harder than ever and almost do the impossible. That's when God decided to step in and take action (Ex. 2).

A Bush on Fire

One day as Moses was taking care of his father-in-law's sheep, he led them past Mount Sinai, searching for better grazing. As he gazed up toward the mountain, he saw a bush on fire, but it didn't burn up. "That's strange," he said to himself. "I'm going up there to get a closer look and see what's happening."

As he got closer, God called to him from the middle of the flames: "Moses!"

Without thinking, Moses stopped and said, "Yes! I'm here!"

"Don't come any closer!" God commanded. "Take your sandals off, because you're walking on holy ground. I am the God of Abraham, Isaac, and Jacob, and I know what My people are going through in Egypt. I have decided to deliver them, so I want you to go back there and lead them out of Egypt to the land of Canaan."

"But, Lord, Pharaoh will kill me!" Moses stammered. "You know that! Besides, who am I to do such a thing?"

"I will go with you," God answered. "I want you to bring My people to this mountain to worship Me."

"When the people ask who sent me, what should I say?"

"Tell them that the 'I Am,' the God whom Abraham worshipped, has sent you and that I have heard their prayers and will deliver them.

"Then go to the king of Egypt and ask him to let My people go. Tell him that I want the Israelites to come to this mountain to worship Me. I know how stubborn he is and that he will not free My people, but I will bring disasters on Egypt. Then he will release them, and they will not leave empty-handed" (Ex. 3).

Back to Egypt

"Lord, suppose the people won't believe me?" Moses persisted. "Suppose they say, 'The Lord didn't talk to you from a burning bush. You just made that up'?"

"Throw your shepherd's rod down!" God ordered.

When Moses did so, it turned into a snake. Then the Lord asked him to pick it up by the tail, and it became a shepherd's rod again.

Next the Lord said, "Put your hand inside your robe and then pull it out." As Moses removed his hand, leprosy covered it. "Do it again," God directed, and the leprosy vanished. "When you do this in front of the people," the Lord explained, "they'll believe you."

Still fearful, Moses came up with another excuse. "Lord, I'm not a good leader or speaker. I can't talk well in front of people. Besides, I've forgotten so much about speaking Egyptian."

"Who made humans' mouths?" God asked him.

Still Moses hesitated. "Lord, please send someone else!" he pleaded.

Displeased with Moses' continued reluctance, the Lord said, "Your brother Aaron has been wondering what happened to you. I'll tell him where you are, and he'll come to meet you. He knows the Egyptian language, and I'll make him your spokesman, but I will explain to you what I want done."

So Moses took the sheep back to his father-in-law and told him what had happened. "You need to obey the Lord," Jethro said, "so take your family with you and go back to Egypt, as He wants you to. May God's peace be with you." Then Moses took his wife and two sons, said good-bye to Jethro, and headed for Egypt. Partway there he decided to send them back home for safety.

Meanwhile, the Lord had spoken to Aaron and let him know where to find his brother. When the two brothers met, they cried out for joy and hugged and kissed each other. After all, it had been a long time since they had seen each other. Moses brought Aaron up to date and then told him about the burning bush, about how God had spoken to him, and about all the other things that had happened on the mountain. Then they went on to Egypt.

When they arrived, Aaron spoke to the people and explained everything that had taken place, including the miracle of the burning bush. When Moses showed them the two signs God had told him to use—the rod turning into a snake and back again, and Moses' arm covered with leprosy and then being whole again, the people believed that God had sent him back to Egypt to deliver them. In gratitude they bowed to the Lord and worshipped Him (Ex. 4).

Pharaoh

Then Moses and Aaron went to Pharaoh and said, "The Lord has spoken to us and told us to honor Him with a pilgrim festival in the wilderness."

"Who is the Lord that I should listen to Him?" Pharaoh demanded. "I will not let your people go!"

They pleaded with him: "Please let us go, or the Lord will punish us for disobeying Him."

"So your people want to worship? They need to get back to work!"

That same day Pharaoh ordered his foremen to stop providing the

Israelites with straw to use in the bricks and to make them find their own straw, but they still needed to produce just as many bricks. The people complained to Pharaoh, saying, "Why are you so cruel to us? Why are we beaten for not manufacturing the same number of bricks when we have to take so much time searching for the straw we need?"

"You want to take time off to worship your God?" Pharaoh snapped. "Take that time to find straw! Get out of here and go back to work!"

So the people turned against Moses and Aaron and blamed them for Pharaoh's attitude.

In turn Moses complained to the Lord, saying, "You sent me here to help the people, but things have gotten worse!"

"Wait and see!" God encouraged. "I am the God of Abraham and have not forgotten the agreement I made with him. Tell the people I will deliver them and take them back to the land I promised Abraham."

Moses reported to the people what the Lord had said, but they didn't believe him.

Then the Lord told Moses to ask Pharaoh again to release His people. But Moses protested, "Lord, if even Your people won't listen to me, why should Pharaoh?"

When Moses still hesitated, the Lord commanded him to take Aaron and go, and said, "I know that Pharaoh will harden his heart and become more and more stubborn, and I will let him do so. I will have to bring judgments on Egypt until he will beg My people to leave.

"When Pharaoh asks you for a miracle to prove that what you're saying about Me is true, give Aaron your shepherd's rod and ask him to throw it down. It will turn into a snake, just as it did before."

So that's what Moses and Aaron did, but Pharaoh was not impressed. He called in his magicians, and they made their rods take on the appearance of a snake. Then Aaron's snake crawled over to the other snakelike rods and swallowed them. Still Pharaoh refused to free the Israelites (Ex. 5:1-7:13).

The Nile

"Pharaoh is very stubborn," the Lord said to Moses. "Tomorrow morning he will go to the Nile to worship. Meet him there and say, 'The God of the Hebrews has sent me to ask you to let His people go, but until now you have refused. I will strike the river with my staff, and the Lord will show you that He is God by turning the water to blood. The river will begin to stink, the fish will die, and the people will not be able to drink from it.' Then give Aaron your shepherd's rod and have him point it over the land of Egypt. All the rivers, ponds, wells, and water in buckets and jars will stink and turn as red as blood." Moses and Aaron did what the Lord said, and that's exactly what happened.

Pharaoh ordered his servants to dig for water by the banks of the river and bring him some buckets of clear water. Then he asked his magicians to do the same thing, and the water in the buckets turned red and began to stink. So Pharaoh ignored what the Lord had done to the river and returned to his palace.

The plague lasted a whole week, and the people had to dig for water by the banks of the river, and those who lived farther away had to dig new wells (Ex. 7:14-25).

Frogs

But Pharaoh didn't change. So the Lord said to Moses, "Visit Pharaoh at his palace and say to him, 'The Lord wants you to let His people go. If you don't, He will cover the land with frogs. They will come out of the river and fill your house, your bedroom, and even your bed, and they will infest the houses of the people, their kitchens, and their pots and pans.'"

Again Pharaoh refused to release God's people. Moses gave Aaron his shepherd's rod and asked him to point it toward the water sources of Egypt. Frogs began hopping out of the Nile, the canals, and ponds all through the country—frogs were everywhere! Then Pharaoh called for his magicians and asked them to produce frogs. They all went outside to a pond near the palace, and when the magicians spoke, out came frogs, just as they had happened with Moses.

Pharaoh dismissed Moses and Aaron and asked his magicians to get rid of the frogs, but they couldn't. So he called Moses and Aaron back and said, "Please ask your God to remove these frogs, and then I'll allow your people to leave."

"Tell us when you want them gone," Moses said.

"By this time tomorrow."

"That's when it will be."

Then Moses and Aaron left the palace and prayed, and the next day the frogs died. The people piled them up, and the stench of rotting frogs was everywhere. When Pharaoh saw that the frogs were dead, he changed his mind and refused to let the people go (Ex. 8:1-15).

Gnats

The Lord spoke to Moses and said, "Take Aaron to Pharaoh. When you get there, give Aaron your shepherd's rod, have him hit the ground, and all across Egypt particles of dust will turn into stinging gnats."

So they went to see Pharaoh and requested freedom for the Israelites.

When he still refused, Aaron hit the ground with the shepherd's rod, and all over Egypt dust particles became stinging gnats, just as the Lord had said.

Pharaoh called in his magicians to do the same thing, but they couldn't. "The God of the Hebrews is doing this," they explained.

But still Pharaoh would not free God's people (Ex. 8:16-19).

Flies

A few days later God directed Moses and Aaron to meet Pharaoh by the Nile and say to him, "Let the people go! If you don't, tomorrow the Lord will send swarms of flies all over Egypt. They will be in the air and crawl all over the ground so that people can hardly walk without stepping on them. But the Lord will not send flies into Goshen, where the Hebrews live." Again, Pharaoh rejected their request, and flies appeared everywhere, just as the Lord had said.

The next day Pharaoh summoned Moses and Aaron. "I will let your people go anywhere to worship your God as long as it's in Egypt. Now, get out of my presence!"

"But the Egyptians will be offended when they see us sacrificing animals," Moses reminded him. "We need to go outside the country to do this. It's what God has asked us to do."

"All right, but don't go too far—and pray for me."

"I will pray for you, and tomorrow the flies will be gone. But don't change your mind."

The next day the flies vanished. But Pharaoh changed his mind and refused to let the Israelites leave the country (Ex. 8:20-32).

Sickness

Next the Lord commanded Moses, "Again seek permission from Pharaoh for My people to go. If he refuses, tell him that tomorrow I will send a disease on all livestock: horses, cattle, camels, donkeys, sheep, and goats."

It happened just as the Lord had said it would. The livestock of the Egyptians sickened and died, but those of the Hebrews stayed healthy (Ex. 9:1-7).

Sores

Then the Lord asked Moses and Aaron to return to Pharaoh, and He said, "Take a handful of ashes with you, and if Pharaoh will not let My people leave, throw the ashes up in the air, and they will turn into a fine dust and spread all over Egypt. Whether this dust settles on a person or on any remaining livestock, it will produce boils that will break out in open sores."

When Moses and Aaron did that, even the magicians broke out in open sores and they would not confront Moses. In spite of all this, Pharaoh did not listen and would not free the people (Ex. 9:8-12).

Hail

So once again the Lord told Moses to confront Pharaoh and declare: "God says, 'So far I have let you and your people live, yet you still don't acknowledge Me and allow My people to go. If you continue to say that the Hebrews cannot worship Me, I will send additional plagues on you and your people, and many of you will die. This time tomorrow you will see a hailstorm such as Egypt has never experienced, and any person or domestic animal who is outside will perish.'" Those who believed what Moses said told their servants to bring their animals inside, while others doubted that anything like that could happen.

The next morning Moses pointed his shepherd's rod toward the sky, and the Lord sent lightning, thunder, wind, and hail. The storm uprooted trees and destroyed crops, except the wheat that had not come up yet, and it killed any servants and animals who had not come inside. But the storm did not disturb the land of Goshen, where the Hebrews lived.

Pharaoh summoned Moses and Aaron and said, "I have sinned! The Lord is righteous! We have done wrong! Pray that this terrible storm will stop, and I will let your people go!"

"As soon as I leave, I will pray and the storm will stop," Moses told him, "and you will know that the earth belongs to the Lord. But I'm afraid that you and your officials don't really believe the storm is from the Lord."

As soon as the storm stopped, Pharaoh and his officials changed their minds again and would not let the people go (Ex. 9:13-35).

Locusts

The Lord again commanded Moses to go to Pharaoh. "I have allowed him to live and be stubborn," God said. "This way My people can tell later generations what I have done for them."

So Moses and Aaron once more went to see Pharaoh. "The Lord wonders how much longer you will hold on to His people," they told him. "Tomorrow He will bring swarms of locusts into Egypt, and there will be so many of them that they will darken the sky and cover the ground. They will eat everything green that's left on the trees and in the field from the previous plagues and will even make their way into people's houses." Then Moses and Aaron turned and departed.

"Your Majesty, how much longer is this man Moses going to cause us all this trouble?" Pharaoh's servants protested. "Our country is nearly ruined. Please let his people go! Why make things worse than they already are?"

So the king had Moses and Aaron brought back to the palace, and Pharaoh said, "I will let your people leave to worship the Lord. Whom do you want to go?"

"Everyone," Moses said, "fathers, mothers, children, and our flocks and herds."

"The men may go, but the rest will have to stay here," Pharaoh objected. "That's final!"

As Moses and Aaron were leaving, the Lord said to Moses, "Point your shepherd's rod out over the land!" When he did, an east wind began to blow and continued the rest of the day and all that night. By morning the sky was black with swarms of locusts, which began to eat everything green that had survived the hailstorm.

Pharaoh sent for Moses and Aaron and said to them, "I have sinned against the Lord and against you. Please forgive me and get rid of the locusts!"

The two Hebrew men departed the palace and prayed. The Lord then sent a strong wind from the west that blew the locusts off the land and into the Red Sea. When the locusts were gone, Pharaoh again forbade the people to go (Ex. 10:1-20).

Darkness

Then the Lord told Moses to point his shepherd's rod toward heaven. When he did, darkness covered the whole country. It was so dark that people couldn't see one another, and it stayed that way for three days, but where the Hebrews lived, there was light.

Pharaoh urgently called for Moses and Aaron and said, "Take your people and worship the Lord. Everyone can go, but you have to leave your flocks and herds behind."

"We need to take our flocks and herds along," Moses replied, "because we don't know which animals the Lord will ask us to sacrifice until we get there."

That really upset Pharaoh, so he told them to get out and said to Moses, "I don't ever want to see your face again! If you ever come back, I'll kill you!"

"As you wish—you will never see my face again" (Ex. 10:21-29).

Death

"I will bring one more disaster on Egypt," God announced to Moses, "and this time Pharaoh will release My people, together with their flocks and herds. Go back to see him, and don't be afraid. I will not let him harm you. Tell him that all the firstborn sons in the country will die, from his own son to those of his servants, as well as those of the workers in the field, even the firstborn of the animals. But the Hebrew sons and their animals will not be touched."

First, Moses met with the leaders of the Israelites and told them what would happen and that soon they would be on their way out of Egypt. He urged the people to visit their masters and neighbors, tell them they were leaving, and ask them for help. By now the Egyptians highly respected Moses and gladly gave the people what they needed, including silver and gold.

Then Moses went to see Pharaoh and related what the Lord had said, adding, "This will happen at midnight all across the country, and when it does, you will be glad to let us go and will even force us to leave." Moses was very angry with Pharaoh as he turned and left (Ex. 11).

Passover

"This month will mark the beginning of your religious year," God announced to Moses. "On the tenth day the father of each family should choose a lamb without defects to be sacrificed four days later. If a family does not have sheep, they may sacrifice a goat. The people are to take the blood and smear it on their doorposts so that when the destroying angel sees the blood, he will pass over that house. The fourteenth of the first month will be a special day throughout your history." The people listened to Moses and did everything that God commanded.

At midnight on the fourteenth day the Lord's angel went through Egypt, and all the firstborn sons died, from Pharaoh's house and his servants down to the prisoners in jail and all the animals. That night a loud cry of pain spread throughout Egypt when people found their firstborn sons dead.

It was still dark when Pharaoh sent for Moses and Aaron. "Get out of my country, and take your people with you and everything they have!" he ordered. "And pray for me!" The people also urged the Hebrews to leave, because they were afraid that they, too, would be killed.

So after eating the Passover meal, the Israelites left the country, and some of the Egyptians decided to go with them. The Hebrews had been strangers in Canaan and slaves in Egypt for more than 400 years. They would never forget the night of their freedom. And all the people, Hebrews and Egyptians, obeyed the Lord and did what Moses said (Ex. 12).

The Firstborn

"All the firstborn sons whose lives were spared and all the first sons yet to be born, including the first male offspring of the animals, belong to Me," the Lord told Moses.

Then Moses spoke to the people and said, "Don't ever forget this day! After you settle in Canaan, a country rich in harvests and natural resources, keep the Passover feast and follow it with a weeklong festival. Rejoice in the Lord and what He has done for you. During this time you are to eat no leavened bread. You should keep this festival at the same time each year, and when your children ask you what all this means, tell them that it began in Egypt when the Lord's angel 'passed over' your houses.

"And when you get to Canaan, don't forget to sacrifice a lamb for your firstborn sons and for the firstborn of your work animals. When your sons ask you why you're doing this, remind them of Egypt and what the Lord did for you. Tell them how stubborn Pharaoh was and how the Lord spared your firstborn sons and set them apart for Him as special" (Ex. 13:1–16).

Leaving Egypt

When the people left Egypt, they took the bones of Joseph with them, as he had asked them to do. The Lord did not take them to Canaan through the land of the Philistines but led them toward the Red Sea. During the day He guided them by a pillar of cloud, and at night He gave them light with a pillar of fire.

"Pharaoh will regret letting you go and will come after you to take you back to Egypt," God told Moses. "He thinks he can do that easily, so I will let him try, and he will find out that I am the Lord."

When Pharaoh realized that the Hebrews had no intention of coming back, he called up his best troops, had them mount 600 chariots, and took off after the Israelites. The Israelites saw the Egyptian army approaching and cried out to the Lord for help. Then they turned to Moses, blaming him, and said, "Why did you bring us out here to die or be killed? We're going back to Egypt with Pharaoh. Just leave us alone!"

"Don't be afraid and make hasty decisions when you see Pharaoh's army," Moses encouraged them. "Just wait, and you'll see what God will do."

"Have the people head toward the Red Sea as quickly as they can," the Lord instructed Moses. "When you get there, point your shepherd's rod toward the water. The sea will separate, and the people will be able to walk across on dry ground."

Then the Lord's cloud moved from the front of the people to the rear, and as it settled on the Egyptian army, the cloud turned so dark that Pharaoh and his men couldn't see one foot ahead of them, yet it was light on the side of the Hebrews. That way the Lord held Pharaoh and his troops back all night until the sea opened and His people could get to the other side.

Moses pointed his shepherd's rod toward the Red Sea, and the sea opened. Then a strong east wind began to blow all night, drying the ground. In the morning the people walked across the sea bed, with walls of water piled up on both sides. As soon as they got across, the cloud behind them lifted and moved in front of them.

When Pharaoh could see the way clear, he and his soldiers raced after the Israelites, but when the army was halfway across, Moses pointed his shepherd's rod toward the Red Sea, and water began seeping up from the ground, turning it into mud. Pharaoh's horses and chariots got bogged down. Although they tried to turn around, they couldn't. Then the walls of water on both sides came crashing down, and Pharaoh and all his men drowned, some of them floating to the surface.

When the people saw what the Lord had done, they greatly feared Him and decided to listen to Moses (Ex. 13:17–14:31).

Song of Freedom

Then Moses and the people sang: "We will sing to the Lord, for the victory is His! He is our strength and song! He is our salvation, our God, and we will praise Him forever!

"Lord, Your right arm is strong and powerful. You have defeated those who were against You. You overthrew their power. The surging waters covered them, and they are gone. They thought they would conquer, take the sword and win. But You spoke to the wind, and the mighty waters swallowed them up.

"Who is like You? Who is like You in power and holiness, doing wonders never before seen? You brought Your people out of Egypt. You redeemed them, and showed them the way to go.

"The nations have heard what You have done, and their courage has fled. They see Your strength and are as silent as stones.

"You will bring Your people to the holy mountain, to the land You promised. You are our King forever!"

Then Miriam, the sister of Moses, took her tambourine and led the women in a joyous dance. Her voice burst forth in song: "Sing to the Lord, for He has triumphed! He has thrown the riders and their horses into the sea!" (Ex. 15:1–21).

seven

Sinai

After the people crossed the Red Sea, the Lord led them to Sinai. On the way they came to an oasis with water, but it tasted bitter, so they blamed it on Moses. He prayed to the Lord for help, and the Lord showed him a small tree and told him to cut it down and throw it into the water. As soon as he did, the water turned sweet.

Then the Lord said, "If My people will listen to Me, do what's right, and keep My commandments, I will heal them as I did this water, and they will not suffer from the diseases of Egypt."

Moses told the people what God had said, and from there the Lord led them to a place with 70 palm trees and 12 springs of water, where they set up camp (Ex. 15:22-27).

Manna

After a short time there, they broke camp and continued on their way to Sinai. By now it had been a month since they left Egypt, and once again they complained to Moses and Aaron about taking them out of Egypt. "Back there," they said, "we had plenty of meat and bread, but out here we're starving and don't have enough to eat!"

"I've heard the complaints of the people," the Lord said to Moses. "Tell them that this evening I will give them meat to eat, and tomorrow morning they will have bread."

Moses reported it to the people, and that evening quails flew in, covering the camp to give them their meat. In the morning, after the dew had evaporated, a small white, flaky substance the size of a pea covered the ground. When the people saw it, they said, "Manna?" meaning "What is this?"

"This is the grain for bread that the Lord promised," Moses explained, "so take what you need for your family, two quarts per person. Don't try to save any for tomorrow, because it won't keep." Some didn't believe him, and what they kept for the next day spoiled and became full of worms. Those who gathered the amount allowed had enough, and those who had collected extra discovered that even then they still had only what they needed.

Every morning the people went out to get manna for their families, and when the sun came up, what remained on the ground then melted. On the morning of the sixth day, they gathered twice as much so that they would have enough for Sabbath, and it did not spoil. Others decided to wait until early Sabbath morning to collect it, but there was none.

The Lord spoke to Moses and said, "How long will these people disobey Me and not believe what I say? The Sabbath is a day of rest." So the people stopped doing their chores, stayed inside the camp, and rested on the Sabbath as God had said.

One morning Moses told Aaron to gather two quarts of manna to keep as a reminder of what the Lord had done for them. Aaron did, and it did not spoil. For 40 years the Lord fed the people with manna, from the time they lived in the wilderness until they settled in Canaan (Ex. 16).

Water

The people continued on their way to Sinai and camped at Rephidim, but the place did not have enough water for them. Again they complained to Moses, saying, "Why did you take us out of Egypt—to kill us? We don't have enough water! Where is the Lord? Has He brought us out here and left us to die?"

Moses pleaded with God. "Lord, what should I do? The people are ready to stone me to death!"

"I know what's going on. Call the people together, and take some of the elders with you to the rock that I will show you. I'll stand on the rock, and when you get there, I want you to strike it with your shepherd's rod. Water will flow out of the rock, enough for the people and their flocks and herds." That's what Moses did, and water began to gush out of the rock, just as the Lord had promised. Then Moses named the place Messah and Meribah, which means "Temptation and Murmuring" (Ex. 17:1-7).

War

The Amalekites decided to attack God's people. Moses said to Joshua, "Quick! Take your strongest men and stop the Amalekites before they enter the camp. I'll go up on the hill with my shepherd's rod and sit on a rock and pray for the Lord to help us." As long as Moses held up his hands in prayer, the Israelites would win, but when he put his hands down, they would lose. Moses got so tired of holding up his arms in prayer that he couldn't do it any longer. So Aaron and Hur stood on each side of him to support his arms. As long as Moses' arms were raised and he prayed, the Hebrews were winning, and by sunset they had defeated the Amalekites.

Then the Lord said to Moses, "Write down what happened so that Joshua and the people won't forget what I have done for them. As a people, the Amalekites will eventually disappear, and no one will remember them."

Moses built an altar there and named it Yahweh Nissi, meaning "God Is Our Banner of Victory!" (Ex. 17:8-16).

Visitors

When Jethro, Moses' father-in-law, heard what God had done to rescue His people from Egypt, he and Moses' wife, Zipporah, and the two children went to find Moses. He was glad to have his family back and told them everything the Lord had done for them, including the hardships they had gone through.

Thrilled at what he heard, Jethro said, "Blessed be the Lord for taking His people out of bondage and delivering them from Pharaoh." Then he offered a sacrifice of thanksgiving to the Lord, and Moses and Aaron, along with the elders, joined him in a sacred meal.

The next day Moses went to work and sat as a judge to settle people's differences. It went on all day from morning to evening until the sun went down. When Jethro saw this, he said to Moses, "What you're doing isn't right. This is too much!"

"But the people are like sheep and need help," Moses explained.

"Your main responsibility is to teach the people and to judge only the most difficult cases," Jethro told him. "You should appoint other judges to handle the smaller cases so people don't have to stand in line all day just to see you. You'll wear yourself out."

Moses listened to his father-in-law and appointed judges, just as Jethro had suggested. He divided the people into groups of 10, 50, 100, and 1,000 and appointed judges over them.

Then Jethro said goodbye and went back home. But Moses' wife, Zipporah, and their two sons decided to stay with the Israelites (Ex. 18).

Sinai

Three months after the Hebrews had left Egypt, they made it to Sinai. Moses went up the mountain to talk with God, and the Lord said to him, "Remind the people of what I have done for them. Tell them that if they listen to Me and do what I say, they will be a special treasure to Me—a kingdom of priests, a holy nation."

Then Moses went back down, called the elders and the people together, reminded them of what the Lord had done for them, and told them what God expected from them. "All that the Lord has said we will do!" they responded. So Moses went back up the mountain and told the Lord what the people had promised.

Then God said to Moses, "The day after tomorrow I will appear over the mountain in a dark cloud and talk to the people. So go back down and tell them to wash their clothes and purify themselves. Mark a boundary line around the mountain, and tell them not to cross it. Anyone who touches the mountain will die, including animals. When they hear the sound of a trumpet, it will be the call to worship." So Moses told the people what the Lord had said.

On the third day, early in the morning, a dense cloud covered the top of the mountain, followed by lightning, thunder, and the sound of a trumpet. The people were afraid, not knowing what to expect. Then Moses led them to the boundary line by the foot of the mountain, while the top of the mountain was on fire. Black smoke rose into the sky, the whole mountain shook, and the trumpet sounded louder and louder. Moses spoke to the Lord, and the Lord answered loud enough for the people to hear, asking Moses to come up the mountain and into the cloud.

They talked for a while, and then the Lord said, "Go back down and remind the people not to try to come up the mountain to see Me."

"They won't," Moses explained, "because we made a boundary line for them not to cross."

"Go down as I asked you to do and warn the people again. Then come back and bring Aaron with you" (Ex. 19:1-24).

The Ten Commandments

After Moses and Aaron reached the top of the mountain, God spoke loud enough for everyone to hear, saying, "I am the one who brought you out of Egypt. These are My commandments:

"You should have no other gods besides Me.

"You are not to make or worship images. If you do, the consequences will follow you down to the third and fourth generations. But if you worship Me and keep My commandments, mercy will accompany you for thousands of generations.

"Don't use My name carelessly, as in taking an oath or in cursing. Those who do so will be punished.

"Remember the Sabbath and keep it holy. You have six days to do all your work, but the seventh day is special. It is holy. No one should work for you on that day, because I created the world in six days and rested on the seventh day and blessed it.

"Respect your father and mother, and you'll live longer.

"Don't kill people.

"Don't commit adultery.

"Don't steal.

"Don't lie.

"Don't be always wanting what others have."

When the people saw the fire and the lightning, and heard the thunder and God's voice, it scared them. "You speak to us for God and we'll listen," they said to Moses. "Don't have God speak to us, because His voice is so powerful it makes us feel as if He's going to kill us."

"You don't have to be afraid of God," Moses told them. "He gave you the commandments because He loves you and doesn't want you to keep on sinning."

But the people were terribly fearful and stood in awe of the mountain.

Then Moses went back up the mountain, and the Lord said to him, "Remind the people not to make images of silver and gold and worship them as the people in Egypt do. When they make an altar for Me on which to offer sacrifices, they are to build it out of natural stone, without tools, and have it sit on the ground, not be high up" (Ex. 20).

Freedom

The Lord continued: "Give the people some practical advice on how to live by the principles of the commandments. Help them understand the underlying principles so that they can apply them to everyday life.

"For example, if a man sells himself as a servant to pay his debts, he is to serve no more than six years. At the beginning of the seventh year, he is free to go—he has fulfilled his obligation. If he did this when he was single, he is to leave single. This will keep female servants still under obligation from marrying him just to secure an early freedom for themselves. If he was married when he sold himself, then he and his family will go free.

"But if he marries while a servant and wants to stay with his wife and loves to work for his master, he should be taken before a judge to confirm his decision. Then his earlobe should be pierced as a sign that he belongs to his master.

"Should a father sell his daughter to be a servant to pay the family debts and the master marries her, the master must treat her as a wife, not as a servant. If the master's son marries her, the same rule applies, and she becomes the master's daughter. Should the son take a second wife, the first one is still his wife, and he should treat her accordingly. If he doesn't, she is free to go and owes him nothing" (Ex. 21:1-11).

Violence

"Whoever is so angry with another person that they could kill that person and hits them with such force that they die," the Lord said, "they must pay for what they have done with their own life. But if they just give the person an ordinary blow and the person still dies, the one who hit the person should be allowed to go to a designated place of safety to live and be protected.

"Whoever strikes their parents or puts a curse on them forfeits their life. Whoever kidnaps someone (male or female), with the idea to sell them or to use them as slaves, is to be executed.

"If during a fight one person hits the other so hard that they knock the person down but nothing serious happens, they are not to be punished. But if the person who got hit is confined to bed and later gets up again to walk with a cane, the one who hit that person is to pay for that person's loss of time and take care of that person until they are well.

"Should someone beat the servants they own and one of them dies, the owner must pay for what they have done. But if the servant gets back to work in a day or two, no payment is necessary, because the servant is the owner's property.

"If a fight breaks out between two people, and a pregnant woman nearby gets accidentally hit trying to help her husband and the baby is born prematurely but neither one is hurt, the one who did it is to be fined an amount the husband decides. But if the result is a serious injury, the person who hit the woman is to be punished according to the law of equality— life for life, eye for eye, or tooth for tooth. "If an owner hits one of their servants in the face, male or female, and the servant loses an eye or a tooth, the owner is to let the servant go free" (Ex. 21:12-27).

Animals

"If a bull or another animal is violent and kills someone, the animal should be killed. However, if the owner knew his animal was dangerous and did not keep it penned up but let it run free, then both the animal and the owner must be put to death, although the owner may redeem their life according to the amount imposed on them.

"If a person's bull or other animal hurts someone else's servant, male or female, and the servant dies, the owner of the animal must pay 30 pieces of silver to the servant's master.

"Should someone's bull attack another person's animal and it dies, the attacking animal must be sold and the profits divided, as well as the meat of the dead animal. If an animal was known to be violent and was not penned up and it kills another animal, the owner must replace the dead animal with a live one and keep the dead animal.

"If someone leaves a pit uncovered or digs a new one and doesn't cover it, and an animal falls in and dies, they must pay for the animal" (Ex. 21:28–36).

Property

"If a person steals an ox or sheep and then sells it or slaughters it for meat for one's self, they must pay for it by giving the owner five oxen or four sheep. If someone is caught stealing an ox, donkey, or sheep for one's self, they should pay for it by giving the owner two such animals. If someone lets their animal graze in a field that is not theirs, they are to pay the owner from the best of their crop or vineyard. If someone is burning grass or weeds in their field and the fire spreads to a neighbor's stacked or standing grain, the one who was careless must restore what was lost.

"If a thief forces their way into someone's house at night and gets hit on the head and dies, the owner is not guilty. But if the thief tries to find a way into a house during the day and the owner sees them and kills them, the owner is guilty of murder.

"If a neighbor agrees to accept a person's valuables for safekeeping and they are stolen, and if the thief is caught, the thief is to pay double. But if the thief is not captured, the neighbor must appear before the judge and take an oath that they are telling the truth and did not just hide the valuables so that they could have them. The judge's decision is final.

"If a person asks a neighbor to take care of their animals while they are gone and an animal gets hurt, dies, or disappears, and the neighbor swears by the Lord that they did not cause it, the owner must accept it. If an animal has been torn to pieces by a wild animal, there is no guilt. But if an animal has been stolen, the neighbor is responsible and must replace it.

"Should someone borrow an animal and it gets hurt and dies, the borrower must replace it. But if the owner was nearby and saw that it was an accident, or if the neighbor had paid for using the animal, there is no guilt" (Ex. 22:1–15).

Morality

"If a man seduces a virgin who is not engaged to be married, he must pay the marriage price and marry her. Even if her father refuses the marriage, the man must still pay.

"If a person has sex with an animal, they both should be put to death. If a woman practices witchcraft, she should be put to death. An Israelite who worships pagan gods and offers sacrifices to them, should be put to death.

"Don't mistreat a foreigner—remember how you suffered in Egypt. Don't mistreat a widow or an orphan. If you do, I will hear their prayers and will let war invade your land, and your men will be killed.

"Should you decide to lend money to someone who is poor to help them get on their feet, you are not to charge them interest. If a poor person gives you something as a pledge that they will pay you back and you find out it's something they really can't do without, you need to give it back to them before the day is over.

"Don't say your God can't be trusted, and don't curse your leaders. Bring the first sample of your harvests as offerings to Me, for they are Mine, just as your firstborn sons and the firstborn of your animals are also Mine.

"You are a holy people to Me, so be careful what you eat" (Ex. 22:16-31).

Justice

"Don't spread rumors and say things about people that are not true or give a false testimony in court. Don't pervert justice by being partial, even if it is to help someone who is poor. And don't contribute to an innocent person's death by making false accusations against them in court, even if they are your enemy.

"If you find a stray cow, donkey, or another animal, return it to the owner, even if it belongs to someone who hates you. If a man's donkey falls under a heavy load, don't just walk by—help get the donkey back on its feet.

"Don't be bribed into doing something wrong, and don't take advantage of the innocent and poor. And as I said before, don't mistreat a foreigner, because you know how you felt when you were slaves in Egypt" (Ex. 23:1-9).

Farms

"The land should rest every seventh year, just as you rest on the seventh day of the week. You can plant and harvest for six years, but during the seventh year, whatever happens to grow by itself on your farms or in your vineyards should be left for the poor and for any wild animals looking for food.

"As for you, work six days and rest the seventh. This also applies to your farm animals and to those who labor for you.

"Listen to Me! Don't ever worship idols or do what you think they're telling you to do—you'll only get hurt" (Ex. 23:10-13).

Festivals

"My people must observe three important festivals each year: the Festival of Bread, which goes along with the Passover; the Festival of

Harvest, which celebrates the beginning of the harvest; and the Festival of Ingathering, when your work for the year is done. I want all men to attend these festivals, along with their families" (Ex. 23:14-19).

God's Promise

Jehovah said to Moses, "I am sending My Angel to bring you into the land I promised to give you. He is the one who brought you out of Egypt and has been guiding you along the way, and He will continue to do so. Listen to Him and do what He says, because He has My name. Don't turn against Him, because He will not overlook sin, nor will He condone rebellion.

"If you listen to Him and do what He says, I will protect you and fight against your enemies. When He brings you into the land, you are not to serve the local gods, but destroy their temples and altars and leave no reminder of them. You are to worship Me, and I will bless your harvests, heal your diseases, and give you a long life.

"Also, I will send hornets ahead of you to drive out your enemies. I will do this a little at a time so that you can gradually take over the land and have time to cultivate it. Otherwise, it will soon fill with weeds, and the wild animals will come to make their homes there.

"Eventually your borders will extend from Egypt in the south to the Euphrates in the north, from the Arabian Desert in the east to the Mediterranean in the west. Don't make a peace agreement with the Canaanites to let them stay in the country and worship their gods, because this will influence you to do what they're doing" (Ex. 23:20-33).

On the Mountain

Then God asked Moses to come partway up the mountain, bringing Aaron and his two sons, Nadab and Abihu, as well as the 70 elders of Israel with him. Before Moses left the camp, he wrote down what the Lord had promised to do for His people and what was expected of them. Then he shared this with the people, and they responded, "All that the Lord has said we will do."

The next day Moses got up early, built an altar at the base of the mountain, and had some men help him sacrifice animals as a peace offering to the Lord. He sprinkled blood on the altar and toward the people, saying, "This blood seals the covenant you just made with the Lord."

Then Moses did as the Lord said and took Aaron, Aaron's two sons, and the 70 elders partway up the mountain. As they looked at the top of the mountain, they saw God's feet standing on a pavement of brilliant blue, as blue as a sapphire stone. They fell on their knees, worshipped the

Lord, and ate the covenant meal that they had brought along, recommitting themselves to the Lord. Then they all went back down to the camp.

Next the Lord asked Moses to come back up the mountain and to bring Joshua with him. Before Moses left, he told the people that Aaron and Hur would be in charge while he was gone. Then Moses and Joshua took some food with them and headed up the mountain, and when they got near the top, a thick cloud began covering it. So they stopped and for the next six days examined their hearts, waiting to be summoned into God's presence. On the seventh day, the Lord summoned Moses up the rest of the way up and into the cloud, which from below looked as if it were on fire. Moses spent 40 days in the cloud, without food or water, miraculously kept alive by the power of God, while Joshua waited for Moses to return (Ex. 24).

The Sanctuary

While Moses was in the cloud, God gave him instructions for a portable sanctuary. He told him how big it should be, what materials to use, and what furniture it should have. The total area was to be enclosed with a white cloth fence and have two courtyards. The inner courtyard was to have an altar and a large basin and two rooms sealed off by colorful curtains. The first room would have a table for holy bread, a candleholder with seven branches, and a small altar for incense. The second room would contain a golden chest with a lid with two carved angels on it (Ex. 25:1-27:21).

The Priests

The sanctuary would need priests. "Take Aaron and all four of his sons, and set them apart for the priesthood," God instructed. "Have long white robes made for them and an extra high-priestly robe for Aaron. His robe should be a blue seamless one with a hole on top for him to put his head through, and there should be golden bells with alternating pomegranates attached to the bottom. He is to wear a chest plate made of cloth with cords, with shoulder straps to hold it in place, and a white headdress like a crown with a golden band for his forehead engraved with the words 'Holy to the Lord.'

"The cloth chest plate should have 12 precious stones in four rows with the name of one of the tribes engraved on each. Also it will have two large gemstones, one on the right and one on the left. When Aaron ministers before Me and has an important question on what he or the people should do, I will answer through one of them.

"Have an ordination service for Aaron and his four sons. Sacrifice a ram for their sins and another ram for their dedication. Take the blood of the second ram and put some of it on their right earlobes, right thumbs, and right big toes, and sprinkle anointing oil on their heads and clothes. The ordination service should be done in stages during seven days.

"Once the sanctuary is built, the priests are to offer a lamb each morning and evening as an act of worship. My presence will make the sanctuary holy, and I will appear between the carved angels on the lid of the golden box. I am the Lord who brought you out of the land of Egypt" (Ex. 28:1-29:46).

Additional Instructions

"Make a small altar out of acacia wood, and cover it with gold. Put it in the first room, and place it in front of the curtain going into the second room. Every morning and evening Aaron is to burn incense on it.

"Also make a large bronze basin and place it in the courtyard between the sacrificial altar and the entrance to the sanctuary. This is so Aaron and the priests can wash their hands and feet before they enter the tent.

"You will need spices for incense. Also, you must make a special oil that you will use to anoint the tent, the furniture, and the utensils, as well as to anoint Aaron and his sons during the ordination service. No one should make such fragrant oil or special incense for themselves.

"I have given Bezalel, the son of Uri, the wisdom to design everything, and have provided Aholiab and those with him the skill to make it. This includes making robes for Aaron and his sons, and the holy oil and spices.

"You will need money for the upkeep of the sanctuary. So have every man 20 years and older bring half a shekel as a ransom offering, the same amount whether they're rich or poor. It is an annual offering as a reminder of what I have done to redeem you from slavery.

"Remind the people to keep the Sabbath, for it is an unchanging sign between them and Me that they are Mine. So they should do all their work during the week, but the Sabbath is a day for rest and worship."

Then the Lord gave Moses two stone tablets on which He had written with His finger the Ten Commandments (Ex. 30:1-31:18).

The Golden Calf

During Moses' long absence on the mountain, the people became restless and said to Aaron, "We don't know what's happened to Moses or to the Lord. We need a different god to lead us."

Aaron gave in to their demands and asked the men and women, as well as their sons and daughters, to bring him their golden jewelry and earrings. When they did, he built a fire, melted the earrings, and from the molten gold he made a little golden calf. Then the people announced, "Listen! This statue will be a reminder of who brought you out of Egypt. Tomorrow we'll have a festival to the Lord!" The next day they brought their animals as offerings, sacrificed them to the little golden calf, and then held a pagan festival with all its immoral practices.

God saw what had happened and said to Moses, "You need to go back down, because the people you brought out of Egypt are worshipping a little golden calf and going through all the immoral fertility rites that pagans do. These people are so stubborn that I'm going to destroy them—and don't try to stop Me! Then I'll make you and your descendants into a great nation."

"No, Lord!" Moses protested. "Everyone knows that it was You who brought the people out of Egypt. What would that do to Your reputation? The nations will say that You rescued them from Egypt just to kill them because they wouldn't listen to You. What would that say about the kind of God You are? And what about the promise You made to Abraham and Isaac and Israel?"

The Lord was testing Moses' love for the people, so He then said to him, "I have listened to you and will not destroy them, but I want you to go down and stop what they're doing."

So Moses took two tablets of stone that God had written His law on, picked up Joshua on the way, and headed down the mountain. Partway down Joshua said, "Listen! I hear shouts coming from the camp. We're being attacked!"

"No," Moses answered, "those are not war cries, but rather loud religious shouting."

As soon as Moses saw the little golden calf and what was going on, he became so angry that he went to the edge of the camp and, in the sight of the people, threw down the stone tablets so hard that they broke into pieces. Then he strode into the camp, took the little golden calf, and threw it into the fire. When it had cooled, he ground it up, poured the powder into some water, and made the people drink it.

Next he turned to Aaron and said, "Why did you let the people do this?"

"Don't be so angry. They thought you'd never come back down, and they wanted a god they could see. So I asked them to bring their golden earrings, and when I threw the earrings into the fire, the gold flowed together into the shape of a calf."

Moses could sense the determination of the people to worship the golden calf, and when he saw Aaron's weakness to stop them, he went to the entrance of the camp and called out: "Whoever is on the Lord's side, come over here!"

All the men from the tribe of Levi joined him. "Take your swords," Moses instructed them, "and go from one end of the camp to the other. Whoever attacks you in order to keep this immoral worship going, kill them."

So that's what the Levites did, and they ended up slaying 3,000 men. Because of the stand the Levites took against such defiant sin, the Lord made the Levites into a tribe of priests and servants of the sanctuary.

Then Moses said to the people, "You need to repent and recommit yourselves to the Lord. I'm going back up the mountain to see what the Lord has to say."

When he got to the top of the mountain, he pleaded with the Lord: "Please forgive these people, and if that's not possible, then take my name out of the book of life."

"Those who don't repent and continue in such open rebellion are the ones whose names I'll take out of the book of life," the Lord replied. "Now go back down and lead the people out of Sinai toward Canaan, and I'll go with you."

Then the Lord sent a plague on the people to discipline them for what they had done (Ex. 32).

Repentance

The Lord said to Moses, "Take the people you brought out of Egypt and lead them on to Canaan. I will go with you and protect the people, but only from a distance. They are still inclined to be stubborn, so I will not appear in their midst as before, because if I did, My presence would destroy them."

When Moses told the people what the Lord had said, they mourned and took off their jewelry as a sign of repentance and renewed obedience. The Lord told them not to wear their earrings and jewelry again to avoid being led back into their previous practices.

Then Moses pitched his tent outside the camp where the Lord was and met with Him there. Whenever Moses went to the sanctuary and the people saw him go, out of respect they would stand at the opening of their tents until he had gone inside, and when the Lord's cloud appeared over the sanctuary, they would bow and worship beside their tents. And whenever the Lord talked to Moses, He would speak to him directly, just as a human being does with a friend.

After this, Moses went back up the mountain and said to the Lord, "You asked me to lead the people to Canaan, but let me know what Your plans are, because these are Your people, not mine. You brought them out of Egypt—I didn't."

"My presence will go with you—I will not leave you."

"How can we know that Your presence will go with us and that You will not turn away from us?"

"I will confirm My promise to you right now by letting you see My presence," God said, "but not My face, because no man can see My face and live. I will make an opening in the rock on which you're standing, put you in it, and cover you with My hand as I pass by. Then I'll take My hand away and let you see My back, but not My face." Then as the Lord's presence passed by, He said, "I will be gracious to whom I will be gracious and have compassion on whom I will have compassion" (Ex. 33).

New Tablets of Stone

The Lord said to Moses, "Go back down and chisel out two stone tablets like the ones I gave you before. Then tomorrow morning, come back up, this time alone, and before you leave camp, warn the people to stay away from the mountain and not to let their animals graze near it, either."

So Moses went down, prepared two stone tablets, and reminded the people of what the Lord had said. The next morning he went back up the mountain by himself, carrying the stone tablets.

When he reached the top, God passed in front of him and said, "I am the Lord, merciful and gracious, patient and kind, and full of goodness and truth. I keep My promises. I forgive sins, but I do not overlook sin."

Moses bowed and said, "Lord, if I have found grace in Your sight, please forgive the people."

"I will do wonderful things for My people that I have not done for any other people," the Lord replied. "I will do things you've never seen before and fight against your enemies to open the way for you to make your way to Canaan. My people are not to make a peace treaty with their enemies, for their enemies will not keep their word. Be sure to destroy their idols and altars so that you won't be tempted to worship as they do. Do not accept an invitation to join them in worship, and don't let your sons marry their daughters, because they will turn their hearts away from Me.

"My people are not to make any kind of images and worship them. They should keep the Passover, followed by the Festival of Bread, as you did when you came out of Egypt, and don't forget that all firstborn males are Mine, including the firstborn from animals. Do all your work in six days, and rest on the Sabbath. Don't overlook the festivals I gave you, especially the three main ones that all men must attend: the Passover, which I mentioned, and the Festival of Pentecost and the Festival of Tabernacles, both of which are harvest festivals. Their families may accompany them, and when they come to worship Me, have them bring an offering, and I will renew my covenant with them. Write these things down so that the people won't forget them."

Then the Lord wrote the Ten Commandments as He had done before, only this time on the new set of stone tablets. When Moses came down, carrying them, his face glowed with the glory of God. Aaron was afraid to approach Moses, but Moses called to him and told him there was nothing to be afraid of. So Aaron went to Moses, and when the leaders of Israel saw this, they came closer and Moses spoke with them. Then the people joined them, and Moses told them everything the Lord had said. Then he put a veil over his face. Whenever he went into the sanctuary to commune with the Lord, he took the veil off, and when he emerged to speak to the people, he would put it back on (Ex. 34).

Building the Sanctuary

Moses reminded the people about the Sabbath and to bring their offerings to the Lord and do so gratefully. He especially asked them to bring gold, silver, and bronze metals; blue, purple, and red cloth; and animal skins, acacia wood, oil, spices, and gemstones for building the sanctuary.

He requested Bezalel, whom the Lord had specially gifted, to draw the plans. And he assigned the craftsmen to begin making tent poles, roof coverings, curtains, an altar, and the various items of furniture for the sanctuary.

Both men and women gave liberally and did all they could to help the craftsmen. In fact, the people brought more than enough so that Moses had to tell them to stop. Then the work began in earnest, and the craftsmen prepared the curtains, clothes for the priests, and all the pieces of furniture needed (Ex. 35:1–39:43).

Dedication of the Sanctuary

When everything was ready, the Lord spoke to Moses and said, "Set up the sanctuary tent on the first day of your religious year. First, put the golden box [the ark] in the second room called the Most Holy Place. Then install the lampstand with its seven branches, the little altar of incense, and the table for the holy bread in the first room, called the holy place. Next, place the sacrificial altar and the large bronze washbasin in the courtyard. Hang curtains at the gate and at the entrance to the rooms, and set up the high curtain fence around the whole sanctuary.

"Consecrate the altar and all the furniture with a touch of the special oil you made. Then bring in Aaron and his sons, put the priestly robes on them, and anoint them with oil."

Moses did everything the Lord said. After the craftsmen had erected the wallboards and draped the roof covers over them, the curtains were hung to divide the sanctuary. Then the furniture was brought in and the altar set up, as were the stakes with the curtains surrounding the sanctuary.

When they had everything done, the cloud of the Lord came down and covered the sanctuary, and the blazing light of His presence filled the place—even Moses couldn't go in.

The Lord's cloud hovered over the sanctuary during the day, and at night it turned into a pillar of fire. When the cloud lifted and moved, the people would break camp and follow it. If it didn't move, the people stayed in the same place (Ex. 40).

eight

Leviticus: Guidebook

The Lord called Moses into the sanctuary and said to him, "Tell the people that when they bring an animal for an offering, it should be a male without flaws. They should take it to the entrance of the sanctuary and wait for the priest to call them in. They should go in and there place their hands on the animal, silently confess their sins, take the knife from the priest, and kill the animal. The priest will do the rest.

"When someone has an offering of oil and flour, the priest is to burn it on the altar, and if the offering includes grain from the field, the grain not used goes to the priest and his family. If it's a bread offering, it should be made without yeast, and when it's presented, the priest should add salt to it, as he does the other offerings. Salt is a preservative and a symbol of the agreement I have made with My people" (Lev. 1:1–2:16).

Various Offerings

Then the Lord explained to Moses the purpose of the different offerings, what those who bring them should do, and how the priests should present them. The peace offering was an expression of gratitude for what the Lord had done or as a commitment to Him and to the mission of Israel. The sin offering was for sins committed, including unintentional ones, because all sin is wrong, and if someone has been hurt by what has been done, restitution needs to be made. The burnt offering was one of dedication to the Lord and should be presented by the priest for the people every morning and evening throughout the year, with additional ones during scheduled festivals. Each type of offering had its own procedure, which the Lord carefully outlined to Moses (Lev. 3:1–7:38).

Consecration of Priests

Next God spoke to Moses about the priests: "I want you to bring

Aaron and his sons into the sanctuary courtyard and consecrate them to Me. Put the priestly garments on them, and anoint Aaron and his sons with oil. Offer a young bull as a sin offering, along with two rams and some bread without yeast for Aaron and his sons. Be sure to do everything I am asking you to do." So this is what Moses did (Lev. 8).

The consecration service lasted for seven days, and on the eighth day Moses authorized Aaron and his sons to begin their priestly ministry. He told Aaron to offer a sacrifice for himself and one for the people, and have them bring their own sacrifices as well. When the people did, Moses and Aaron blessed them (Lev. 9).

Disobedience

Two of Aaron's sons, Nadab and Abihu, did not follow the Lord's instructions on what to do in the sanctuary. They took their censers and, under the influence of wine, put ordinary fire in them instead of sacred fire from the altar that the Lord had lit. Then they added incense, and as they went into the sanctuary to wave the incense before the Lord, fire flashed out from the presence of the Lord and struck them dead.

"Your sons used unauthorized fire and did not obey the Lord," Moses explained to Aaron. "That's why they died." Then he called for the Levites to carry out the bodies and told Aaron and his remaining two sons, Eleazar and Ithamar, not to tear their priestly robes as a sign of grief, and that if they left the sanctuary to attend the funeral, they, too, would die. The rest of the family could take care of their brothers' burial.

Then the Lord spoke to Aaron and said, "Your sons had been drinking fermented wine, which affected their judgment. No one who serves at the sanctuary—priests or Levites—should drink anything intoxicating, or they will die. They need to have clear minds to know the difference between what is sacred and what isn't."

Moses reinforced what the Lord had said and gave Aaron and his two remaining sons specific instructions about the procedures to follow when offering sacrifices to the Lord. They were to eat only from the leftover grain offerings and those parts of the sacrifices belonging to the priests and their families. Later that day, they forgot, and Moses had to reprimand them.

Apologizing, Aaron said, "This has been a very hard day for us. My sons, Eleazar and Ithamar, did forget to do some things right, but surely the Lord will accept the sacrifices we offered, considering what we've been through today."

When Moses heard that, he understood their grief, and was satisfied (Lev. 10).

Health Laws

The Lord was also concerned about the health of His people. "I want My people to be healthy," he said to Moses, "so they need to be careful what they eat. Acceptable meat is from animals that have split hooves and chew the cud such as the cow, but not from those such as the pig, which has a split hoof but does not chew the cud, or the camel, which chews the cud but does not have a split hoof. You should follow the same criteria when choosing meat from other animals.

"As for fish, you can eat those that have both fins and scales, but not the rest. Don't eat scavenger birds, such as eagles, falcons, ravens, hawks, owls, ostriches, or storks. And do not eat insects that crawl or walk, only those that jump, like the grasshopper. Leave the rest alone.

"Don't eat animals that died on their own. You don't know what sickness they had or what else may have caused them to die. And don't drink contaminated water.

"I want My people to be healthy and holy, for I am holy. That's the reason I brought them out of Egypt, so they need to be careful what they eat" (Lev. 11).

Disease and Cleanliness

The Lord continued, "When a woman has a baby, she should take care of herself. For 33 days for a boy or 66 days for a girl, she should stay at home and not come to the sanctuary. After that, she should bring a lamb and a pigeon for an offering. If she can't afford a lamb, two pigeons will do.

"When anyone has a skin disease, they should have the priest look at it to see if it's the beginning of leprosy. If it looks like leprosy, they should be isolated for a week and then be reexamined. If it's not leprosy, they may go home. But if it is, they should wear a torn robe and not comb their hair so that others can see that they are sick, and they should live outside the camp until cured. All skin diseases should be carefully examined.

"When someone is cured, they should follow the procedure for purification as outlined by the priest. A man should shave his beard, take a bath, and put on clean clothes. Then he should bring two sparrows, two lambs, some grain, and two young pigeons and follow the procedure as outlined by the priest.

"If mildew is suspected to be found in a house or on clothes, a priest should inspect it. If he thinks it is mildew, he should ask the people to wash it off and then wait a week to see if it comes back. If it returns, they should burn the mildewed clothes and remove any mildewed bricks or stones and take them to the city dump.

"When a man has an unexpected discharge of semen, he should take a bath, put on clean clothes, and wash the soiled ones. Then he should bring an offering to the sanctuary and follow the instructions of the priest. When a woman's menstrual cycle is longer than it should be or comes unexpectedly, she should keep herself clean and not be sexually active during that time. After her menstrual cycle, she should bring an offering to the sanctuary as specified by the priest" (Lev. 12:1-15:33).

Day of Atonement

After the death of Aaron's two sons the Lord told Moses, "I want you to inaugurate an annual Day of Atonement when the deeds of the previous year are judged. It is a day for My people to reexamine their lives, a time for spiritual renewal and recommitment to Me.

"Aaron should not come into the Most Holy Place except on the Day of Atonement. My presence will be in the small white cloud between the angels on the golden ark. He should have a young bull ready to sacrifice for a sin offering and a ram for the regular daily offering before he enters the Most Holy Place.

"Furthermore, he should wash himself and put on his regular priestly robe and white turban. The tribal leaders are to bring him two male goats for a sin offering and a male sheep for a regular daily offering. Then Aaron should take two stones and mark one 'For the Lord' and the other 'To Be Sent Away.' He should cast lots and then take the Lord's goat and sacrifice it for the sins of Israel and have someone be ready to take the other goat into the wilderness to die.

"Aaron should sacrifice the young bull for his own sins, offer incense on the little altar in the holy place, and then take a sample of the blood into the Most Holy Place. He should sprinkle it seven times on the lid of the ark, called the mercy seat, and seven times in front of the ark. Then he should go back out and offer the Lord's goat to make a cleansing atonement for the sanctuary because of all of the sacrifices the people brought for their sins throughout the year. No one else should be in the sanctuary at that time.

"After this, Aaron should go to the courtyard and put some of the blood of the bull calf and the Lord's goat on the horns of the sacrificial altar. Next, he should lay his hands on the head of the live goat, putting all the blame for sin on the scapegoat before he sends it into the wilderness to die.

"When the scapegoat has been taken away, Aaron should go back into the holy place, take off his regular priestly robe, wash himself, and put on his high priest's robes. Then he should go out into the courtyard and offer the expected daily sacrifice as a sign of the beginning of a new year.

"The man who led the live goat into the wilderness to die should wash himself before he returns to camp. The bodies of the sacrificed young bull and the Lord's goat should be taken outside the camp and burned.

"The Day of Atonement is to be held on the tenth day of the seventh month of your religious year. No work should be done on that day. It is a day for self-examination, fasting, and prayer.

"When Aaron dies, the annual Day of Atonement is to continue, and the next high priest should do the same things Aaron has done. This day points forward to the time when God will provide a sacrifice for sin and to the time when Satan and sinners will be no more" (Lev. 16).

False Worship

"Tell Aaron and the people," the Lord continued, "that no one should kill an animal and offer it as a sacrifice to Me away from the sanctuary, whether they do it in the camp or out in the field. This could lead to worshipping other gods and pagan practices. If anyone does this, they are no longer considered part of Israel. This rule also applies to foreigners who choose to live among you.

"No one is to drink blood or eat it with other food as pagans do. Blood is sacred and is a symbol of redemption. Even the meat you eat is to be drained of blood. If anyone eats the meat of an animal found dead, they are to wash themselves and their clothes before they come to worship Me" (Lev. 17).

Morality

The Lord said to Moses, "Tell the people of Israel and the foreigners living among you not to practice sex as they do in Egypt or in Canaan. Family members are not to have sex with each other or with in-laws.

"No one should marry the sister of a wife who is still living, lest it cause a rivalry. A man should not have sex with his neighbor's wife, with another man, or with an animal. The land of Canaan is morally sick and ready to vomit out its inhabitants because of such wicked things—that is why I'm driving them out. Don't do such things when you get there, or I'll have to expel you also. Anyone who does such things is not part of My people. Israel is to live by My commandments, for I am their God" (Lev. 18).

Holy Living

"Speak to the people that they should be holy, because I am holy.

Don't worship idols, but do keep the Sabbath and respect your parents. Bring offerings to Me with a willing heart. Don't reap every corner of your field or pick every last grape from your vines—leave some for those who are poor. Don't cheat your neighbor or hold back wages from those who work for you, but pay your employees and servants on time. Don't curse those who are deaf or get in the way of those who are blind. Judges should not be partial, whether people are rich or poor. Don't lie or deceive, and don't spread false rumors. Don't harbor hatred in your heart for your neighbor, but love them as yourself.

"When you get into Canaan, don't do what the people around you are doing, such as practicing witchcraft, eating meat with blood in it, shaving their heads, cutting themselves, or being tattooed.

"Don't mistreat those who are elderly or discriminate against the foreigner who has chosen to live among you. Be honest in everything you do, using honest measurements, weights, and scales.

"Do all this and keep My commandments, because I am the Lord" (Lev. 19).

Penalties

"If anyone sacrifices a newborn baby to an idol, they should be executed. Those who practice witchcraft and say they are communicating with the dead are no longer part of My people. Those who put a curse on their fathers or mothers should be executed. If a man commits adultery with his neighbor's wife and she consents, both should be put to death. If a man commits adultery with his mother, his father's second wife, or with his daughter-in-law, even though she consents, both should be executed. Should a man have sex with another man, both should be put to death. And if a man marries a mother and her daughter, all three should be executed.

"If a man has sex with an animal, both he and the animal should be killed. It's the same if a woman does this. If a man marries his sister just to have sex with her, even if she's the daughter of his father or his mother from a previous marriage, both are no longer part of Israel. If a man has sex with a woman during her menstrual cycle and she agrees, both are no longer to be considered as part of My people. If a man has sexual relations with his aunt on his father's side or his mother's side and she consents, I will see to it that they have no children. Don't be influenced by Canaanite culture. Keep My commandments so that I don't have to drive you out of the land, as I'm having to do to them.

"You are a nation set apart, and you belong to Me. So be holy, because I am holy" (Lev. 20).

Conduct of Priests

Then the Lord spoke to Moses about the priesthood: "Tell Aaron and his sons not to get involved in doing funerals or participating in burials, unless the person who died was a member of their family. Handling dead bodies detracts from what priests represent and from what they are appointed to do. When they mourn, they are not to shave their heads or cut their bodies to show grief, as the Canaanites do.

"A priest should not marry a divorced woman or one who has been a prostitute. It's the same for the high priest, and, in addition, he is not to marry a widow, only a woman who is a virgin.

"No one who has physical defects should become a priest. If he belongs to a priestly family, he can eat from the sacrifices and offerings given to support the priesthood, but he is not to minister in the sanctuary and approach the altar to offer sacrifices. I, the Lord, decide those who are to serve Me, so they need to be holy as I am holy.

"Tell Aaron and his sons to show respect for the offerings the people bring, because those offerings belong to Me. No priest is to offer sacrifices for the people if he has a physical defect, because he represents Me. If a priest gets sick, has an infectious disease, or has touched a dead body, he should not come near the altar to offer sacrifices until he is well and has cleansed himself.

"No one except the priest's family is to eat from the sacrifices given to support the priest, not even his servants or houseguests. When a priest's daughter gets married, she should not expect to continue to receive part of those sacrifices unless she becomes divorced or widowed and returns home to live.

"Aaron and his sons are not to accept as offerings animals that are defective, inferior, stunted in growth, or deformed. Newborn animals shall stay with their mothers for seven days before being brought to Me as offerings.

"People should show respect for Me and bring their offerings willingly, not grudgingly. I am the Lord who brought them out of Egypt" (Lev. 21:1–22:33).

Festivals

The Lord continued speaking to Moses. "There should be six festivals each year besides the weekly Sabbath. The fourteenth day of the first month of your religious year is the Lord's Passover, which is immediately to be followed by the weeklong Festival of Unleavened Bread. Fifty days later, at the beginning of the wheat harvest, the people are to celebrate a one-day Harvest Festival, to be known as Pentecost. In the seventh month you will have the one-day Festival of Trumpets. It is the beginning of 10 days of preparation for the Day of Atonement, when everyone will be judged for their deeds during the past year. Five days after the Day of Atonement, people should celebrate the Festival of Shelters and the final harvest by making booths for themselves and camping in them for a week. It is to be a reminder of their freedom and of how they lived when I first brought them out of Egypt.

"The first and last days of the weeklong festivals (Festival of Unleavened Bread and Festival of Shelters) are to be special Sabbaths, during which no regular work should be done. At these festivals the people are to bring their offerings, whether it be animals or samples of the firstfruits and grain harvests. The priests are to offer the appropriate sacrifices for each of these occasions" (Lev. 23).

Important Rituals

Then the Lord talked to Moses about items in the sanctuary and said, "Only pure olive oil should be used for the seven-branched lampstand. The lamps should be kept burning day and night to remind people of My continuous presence.

"Twelve loaves of flat bread should be placed on the little bread table in the holy place in two stacks of six. Each Sabbath they should be replaced with fresh bread" (Lev. 24:1-9).

Justice

The Lord continued, "If a foreigner who lives among you and an Israelite get into an argument, and the foreigner curses the God of Israel and the people hear it, the man should be tried. If he is found guilty, he should be executed. This applies to foreigners and Israelites alike.

"Whoever kills another person should be put to death, and whoever kills an animal belonging to another should replace it. If anyone injures another person, breaks a bone, puts an eye out, or knocks out some teeth, the same thing should be done to them. This law applies to everyone, Israelite and foreigner alike" (Lev. 24:10-23).

Special Years

Next the Lord spoke to Moses about the sabbatical year and the year of jubilee. "Every seventh year the fields and orchards should rest," God said. "There should be no regular sowing or reaping that year. Whatever grows on its own is for you, your family, your servants, and the foreigners living among you. It is for your animals and for the wild animals roaming your land.

"The forty-ninth year is also a sabbatical year, and the year following is the year of jubilee, which is a year of freedom and liberty and a year of returning property to its original owners. No property is permanently sold, but when it is sold, its value is to be determined by the number of years remaining before the next jubilee" (Lev. 25:1-24).

Debts

"If a person falls on hard times and becomes poor, you should help them, whether they're an Israelite or a foreigner living among you. Don't make money off anyone who is in debt by charging interest. If they are so far in debt that they couldn't possibly pay you back, they can work it off by becoming your servant but only until the year of jubilee. At that time you must let them go free.

"Don't take advantage of someone and their family. Remember the treatment you received in Egypt and how you didn't like it.

"If foreigners sell themselves to an Israelite, it is to be permanent. Foreigners are not to take advantage of your kindness with a plan to leave Israel. But if Israelites sell themselves to rich foreigners living among you, they serve only on a year-to-year basis. Their family and relatives can redeem them according to the years left until the year of jubilee. If no one redeems them, when the year of jubilee does come, they are to go free" (Lev. 25:35-55).

Blessings Are Conditional

"Do not make images and worship them. I am the Lord your God. Don't forget that I am the one who brought you out of Egypt, so keep My Sabbaths and respect My sanctuary.

"Obey Me, and keep My commandments, and I will bless you. I will give you sunshine and rain, your crops will grow, and your vineyards and trees will be full of fruit. I will protect you, the land will have peace, and you will sleep without being afraid. If your enemies decide to attack, five of you will chase away 100, and 100 of you will put 10,000 to flight. I will walk among you and be your God, and you will be My people.

"But if you do not obey and keep My commandments, there will be no peace. Disease will sweep through the land, and your enemies will take your crops and eat your fruit. And should you continue to disobey Me, I will let your enemies attack your cities, and they will surround you and cut off your food supply to starve you out. You will be so hungry that you will take the lives of your newborn babies and eat them just to stay alive. Your enemies will destroy your cities, take some of you captive, and scatter the rest of you. That will be the end of you as a nation.

"But if you confess your sins and decide to obey Me, I will remember the covenant I made with your ancestors, bring you back home, and once again bless you.

"I am the Lord who brought you out of Egypt" (Lev. 26).

Vows

Again the Lord spoke to Moses and said, "Tell the people that if a man, while under stress of circumstances, vows to do something for Me, which may include his wife and children, and the situation changes so that he can't do it, he should bring a gift to redeem his vow. The gift is to be calculated as follows: for an adult male, 50 shekels; for an adult female, 30 shekels; for a young male, 20 shekels; for a young female, 10 shekels; for little boys, 5 shekels; for little girls, 3 shekels; for old men, 15 shekels; and for old women, 10 shekels. If the men or women are too poor to redeem the vow, they should go to the priest, who will adjust the payment according to what they can afford.

"If someone promises to give Me a certain animal as a sacrifice, another animal cannot take its place. If all that someone has is an animal not suited for sacrifice, such as a donkey, he should take it to the priest, who will sell it and put the money in the offering. But if the owner doesn't want his animal sold, he can buy it back for the price the priest set, plus 20 percent, and the animal will be his again.

"This same rule applies to someone who promises to give Me his house or a piece of land. If a person sells a piece of property and promises to give it to Me, that property cannot be bought back. It would be like double-dealing. All land is really Mine.

"One tenth of all produce and animals belongs to Me. The owner is not to line up his animals in such a way that a sickly one is Number Ten. He is to let the animals push through the gate in single file, and every tenth one is Mine, even if it is a prized one. No other animal can be substituted."

These were the rules the Lord gave Moses at Sinai for the people (Lev. 27).

nine

Numbers: The Journey

In the second year after Israel left Egypt, the Lord said to Moses, "Count the people by tribes and families, numbering the men 20 years and older who are fit for military service, and ask the tribal leaders to help you."

The largest tribe was Judah, and the smallest was Manasseh. Among all the tribes more than 600,000 men qualified for military service. But the tribe of Levi was not included, because their responsibility was to take care of the sanctuary and the spiritual needs of the people.

Then the Lord told Moses how to set up camp as the people moved from place to place. "The sanctuary," God said, "is to be in the center of the camp with the entrance facing east so that when the people come to worship Me, the sun will be to their backs.

"The tribes of Judah, Isaachar, and Zebulun should pitch their tents to the east; Reuben, Simeon, and Gad, to the south; Ephraim, Manasseh, and Benjamin, to the west; and Dan, Asher, and Naphtali, to the north." And the people did everything the Lord said (Num. 1:1-2:34).

The Levites

Aaron had four sons: two of them had died, while serving as priests, and had no children. But the other two, who also served as priests, did have children, and it was through them that the Aaronic priesthood continued.

The Lord said to Moses, "The tribe of Levi is to assist Aaron and his sons in attending to the needs of the sanctuary and the people. I have taken the Levites to be Mine in place of the firstborn whose lives I spared in Egypt. Number the Levites, making a list of all males from 1 month old and up."

Jacob was the father of Levi, who had three sons, and each of them had sons. There were more than 22,000 Levites from 1 month old and up, but much less than the firstborn who had been spared in Egypt. Then the

Lord said to Moses, "You must pay a redemption price of five silver coins for each of the firstborn over and above the number of Levites. Give this money to Aaron to use for the sanctuary."

God next asked Moses to list all able-bodied Levites from 30 to 50 years of age and divide the responsibilities of caring for and transporting the sanctuary according to clans. Aaron and his sons were to supervise everything. The census found more than 8,000 Levites available to serve the tabernacle (Num. 3:1-4:49).

Community Rules

"Everyone who has leprosy or a contagious disease, men and women," God said, "should live outside the camp so that no one else gets sick.

"If a person has done something that has brought a loss to someone, they should confess their sin to the Lord and repay the loss plus 20 percent. If the victim is dead with no close family members left, the restitution should be given to the priest. In addition, a ram should be sacrificed for what was done.

"If a man's wife has been unfaithful and has kept it a secret and her husband suspects something, he is to bring her to the priest, together with a grain offering. The priest is to take a little bowl of water, sprinkle some dust from the floor of the sanctuary into the bowl, and have her stand before the altar. He is to uncover the woman's head, loosen her hair, and ask her to take the grain offering in her hands while he holds the water. Then he is to say to her, 'If you have not committed adultery, this water won't hurt you. But if you have, your womb will shrink, your abdomen will swell, and you will live with pain for the rest of your life.' Then the woman should drink the water. If she has committed adultery and kept it a secret, the priest's prediction will come true, and she will bear the consequences of her sin" (Num. 5).

Special Consecration

The Lord continued, "If a man promises to set himself apart for Me in a special way for a specific number of days, he should not eat or drink anything made from grapes during that time. He should not shave or touch a dead body, not even to help prepare a family member for burial.

"When the special days are over, he should come back to the sanctuary with the necessary offerings. The man should shave his head and burn the hair on the altar, together with the man's offerings.

"Whatever the man promised to do for the Lord during this special time should be done" (Num. 6:1-21).

A Priestly Blessing

The Lord said to Moses, "This is what Aaron and his sons should say when they bless the people: 'The Lord bless you and keep you. The Lord make His face to shine upon you, and be gracious to you. The Lord look upon you with favor and give you peace.' When they do this, I will bless the people" (Num. 6:22-27).

Tribal Leaders

After Moses had set up the sanctuary and anointed the furnishings and the altar, the leaders were the first to bring their gifts. They brought 12 oxen and six covered carts full of gifts, two oxen to pull each cart.

"Accept these gifts," God said to Moses, "and give them to the Levites to help them transport the sanctuary." Moses divided them among the Levites according to their responsibilities.

In addition, each tribal leader brought one silver platter and one silver bowl each, together with oil, flour, and grain, and one gold dish with incense. And each brought the following offerings: a young bull, a male sheep, and a 1-year-old lamb for the burnt offering; one kid goat for a sin offering; and two oxen, five male sheep, five male goats, and five 1-year-old male lambs for a peace offering (Num. 7:1-88).

Dedication of Levites

When Moses went into the Most Holy Place to talk with God, the Lord spoke to him from between the angels and said, "Tell Aaron to make sure that the seven oil lamps attached to the lampstand are toward the front to light up the holy place.

"And tell the Levites to get ready to be dedicated. They should shave, wash their clothes, and make sure their bodies are clean. You should sprinkle them with the water of purification, and a young bull should be sacrificed as a burnt offering, together with flour mixed with olive oil. Another young bull should be sacrificed as a sin offering.

"Have the Levites stand in front of the sanctuary, and have the people watch. The tribal leaders should place their hands on the heads of the Levites, and Aaron will dedicate them as a gift from the people to Me in place of the firstborns I spared in Egypt. The Levites should put their hands on the heads of the two young bulls, one for a sin offering and the other for a burnt offering."

So the Levites prepared themselves for the dedication, and Moses and Aaron and the people dedicated them to the Lord.

Then the Lord said to Moses, "The Levites should perform their assigned duties from the age of 25 to 50 and then retire. After that, they can help as they are able, but they should not be expected to do any of the heavy work" (Num. 7:89-8:26).

The Second Passover

"It has been almost a year since I brought the people out of Egypt," the Lord told Moses one day. "They need to continue to celebrate the Passover as a reminder of what I have done for them. This will be their second Passover, the first one outside of Egypt." So on the fourteenth day of the first month of the new year the people kept the Passover, as the Lord had specified.

Some of the men could not participate in the Passover because they had handled a dead body. They wondered why they had been forbidden, but Moses didn't know, so he asked the Lord.

"Those who have to bury someone or who must be away should still celebrate the Passover wherever they are but not on the same day," the Lord said. "If a foreigner living among you wants to participate, he is welcome to do so" (Num. 9:1-14).

Silver Trumpets

After the sanctuary was set up, a pillar of cloud would settle over it during the day, and at night the cloud would turn into a pillar of fire. When the cloud moved, the people broke camp and followed it, and when it stopped, the people pitched camp.

The priests used silver trumpets to signal the people what to do. Long blasts on both trumpets were a call for the people to assemble at the sanctuary, a long blast on one trumpet was a summons for the tribal leaders to come, short blasts meant it was time to break camp and get ready to move, and shorts blasts a second time were the signal for the tribe of Judah to move out and lead the way.

During times of war the trumpets would signal an attack and announce the time for battle. For festivals the trumpets would let the people know when to bring their offerings (Num. 9:15-10:10).

Breaking Camp

On the twentieth day of the second month, the cloud over the sanctuary lifted and led the people away from Sinai. Whenever they broke camp to travel on, the tribe of Judah was first, and the rest of the tribes followed in assigned order.

Moses invited Hobab, his brother-in-law, to come along. But Hobab said, "I've been with you more than a year now. I'd better go back to see how things are at home." Moses begged him to come with them.

So the people left Sinai, following the cloud, with the priests leading the way and carrying the ark. When the priests picked up the ark, Moses would say, "Scatter our enemies, Lord!" And when the people pitched camp, he would declare, "Come, stay with us, Lord!" (Num. 10:11-36).

The People Complain

Some among the Israelites had married Egyptians and lived on the edges of the camp. They constantly complained, saying, "Why did we ever follow the Lord out of Egypt? In Egypt we had fish, meat, melons, cucumbers, onions, garlic, and more, and ate all we wanted. Now all we have is manna, these granules of white flour that we have to bake."

When the Lord heard this, He was hurt, and so was Moses. "This complaining is more than I can take," Moses told God. "Now they're blaming me for everything! They keep saying, 'Give us meat! Give us meat!' Where am I going to get enough meat to feed all these people? Please end my life—I'd rather die! I can't take it anymore—it's too much for me!"

"I want you to choose 70 men from among the leaders of Israel and have them meet Me here at the sanctuary," the Lord answered. "I will take some of the power of the Holy Spirit I have provided you and give it to them so that they can help you carry the load of leadership. Then tell the people to consecrate themselves, because tomorrow I will give them meat—this time all they can eat for a whole month. They will eat so much meat that they'll get sick of it."

"There are more than 600,000 men, not counting women and children. Even if we killed all our sheep and cattle, we wouldn't have enough to give them meat for a whole month!" Moses said.

"Is anything too hard for Me?" God questioned.

So Moses chose 70 men from among the leaders of Israel and told the people what the Lord had said. When they came to the sanctuary, the Lord gave them some of the power of the Holy Spirit that Moses had earlier received, and they began to prophesy and to praise the Lord. A young man came running to Moses and told him that two of the chosen leaders had not considered themselves worthy to come to the sanctuary but were still in camp, yet they, too, had begun to prophesy and to praise the Lord.

"You need to stop these two men from prophesying and praising the Lord in camp, or it will get out of hand!" Joshua protested to Moses.

"You don't have to defend my leadership," Moses told him. "I wish that all our people had the power of the Holy Spirit." Then Moses and the leaders went to their tents, praising the Lord.

Suddenly a strong wind began to blow in from the west. It brought in thousands of quail, flying about three feet off the ground. The people caught quail all that day, into the night, and all the next day. They stripped them of their feathers and cleaned them for cooking. What they did not immediately use they spread out in the desert sun to preserve by drying. The people soon collected enough quail meat to last them a month. But some couldn't wait and ate large quantities of the meat. Because of their gluttony, the Lord let them get sick, and many people died. They named the place "Graves of Craving." Finally, the people broke camp and went on their way (Num. 11).

Moses' Sister

Moses had married Jethro's daughter when he was in Midian. And Moses' sister, Miriam, had criticized him for marrying someone of a different group of people instead of a Hebrew, and so did Aaron. "Has God spoken only through Moses?" she questioned. "Has He not also spoken through my brother Aaron and me?" Moses was very humble and meek when not called to exercise his leadership in times of crisis, and when he heard Miriam's and Aaron's criticism, he said nothing.

The Lord knew what Aaron and Miriam had grumbled about Moses, so He called the three of them to the sanctuary, and when they arrived, he asked Aaron and Miriam to step forward. Then He said to the two of them, "When I speak through prophets, I do it through visions and dreams, but I speak to Moses face to face, and you think you have the same authority as he has?"

Then the Lord's cloud left the sanctuary, and leprosy suddenly covered Miriam. When Aaron saw this, he was shocked and cried out to Moses, "Don't punish us for our foolishness! Look at Miriam! She already looks half dead!"

Moses pleaded with the Lord to take her leprosy away.

"When a father spits in the face of his daughter to show his disapproval of her wickedness," the Lord said, "she has to repent and live outside the camp for one week. Miriam has done wickedly and has led her brother Aaron to side with her, so let her repent and remain outside the camp for those seven days."

The people waited until Miriam was well and back with them before they broke camp and moved on (Num. 12).

Exploring the Land

After this, the Lord directed Moses, "Choose 12 men, one from each tribe, to explore the land of Canaan where I am taking My people."

Moses selected the men and sent them to find out more about the land of Canaan—its people, their cities, and its soil—and to bring back a report.

He told them not to be afraid but to take courage in the Lord and bring back a sample of what grew there.

The men headed north into the mountains and were gone for 40 days. In the valleys they found large vineyards with huge clusters of grapes. They cut off one large cluster, and it was so big and heavy that they had to hang it from a pole so that two men could carry it. They also brought back samples of other fruit, such as pomegranates and figs.

When they returned and Moses saw the huge cluster of grapes and other fruit, he was amazed. "We explored the land as you told us to," the men said, "and this is the kind of fruit they grow there. Everything is big, even the people. Their warriors are giants, and their cities are well fortified. There's no way we can defeat those people."

Word spread throughout the camp, and the people became scared. Again they blamed Moses for bringing them out of Egypt to face the Canaanites. Then Caleb, who had been with the others, stood up, quieted the people, and said, "We can take the land! The Lord will help us!" And Joshua, who had been with Caleb, said the same thing.

But the other 10 men had discouraged the people. "We can't possibly take the land," they wailed. "Canaan is a very wild country. Besides that, the people are giants. They are so big and strong that we felt like grasshoppers. We'll never defeat them" (Num. 13).

Rebellion

When the people heard this, they wept and said, "If only we had died in Egypt or at Sinai, rather than coming here to be killed by the sword and our women and children becoming victims of war. Let's choose another leader and go back to Egypt!"

Moses and Aaron fell on their knees and pleaded with the Lord to do something. Joshua and Caleb confronted the people and said, "Canaan is a good land—we saw it ourselves. The Lord will give it to us just as He promised. Don't be afraid and rebel against Him—He's with us!" But the people wouldn't listen. In fact, they picked up stones and were ready to kill Caleb and Joshua.

Suddenly the dazzling light of the Lord's presence appeared above the sanctuary. He spoke to Moses and said, "How much longer do I have to put up with these people? Will they ever trust Me? Haven't I given them enough evidence of what I can do for them? I will wipe them out with a pestilence and start over with you and your descendants."

"Lord, You brought these people out of Egypt," Moses protested, "and everyone knows it. The word has spread to other nations, and they talk about what You did to free us and how You led us by a cloud during the day and a pillar of fire by night. Now, if You kill the people, what will the nations say? They'll claim that You couldn't do what You promised. Please forgive our people, Lord, as You have forgiven them before."

"I will forgive them as you asked, but as surely as I live, I will not bring this generation into Canaan. They have seen all the miracles I did for them, but still they don't believe Me. Turn the people around and take them back into the wilderness toward Egypt and the Red Sea. Not one of these complaining people will go into Canaan except their children and Caleb and Joshua, who have a different spirit and believe what I say. Everyone 20 years old and up who didn't trust Me will die and be buried in the wilderness. This will take 40 years, one year for each day that the men explored the land."

Then the Lord struck the 10 men who had given an exaggerated negative report with a plague, and they died.

When Moses told the people what God had said and they saw what happened to those men, they acknowledged their sin and determined to seize the land of Canaan by force. Moses tried to stop them. "Don't rebel again! Don't try to do it now, or the Lord will not be with you!"

But they wouldn't listen. Many of them marched toward the hill country, only to encounter the Canaanites, who swooped down from the mountains and drove the children of Israel back into the wilderness (Num. 14).

Worship, Offerings, and Dress

"Speak to the people for Me," the Lord told Moses, "and say to them, 'When you come into Canaan, you should follow the same procedures for offerings that you were given earlier. These rules and regulations apply not only to you, but also to strangers and foreigners who live among you.'"

"Also tell the people what to do when they sin: 'If you break a law or regulation unintentionally, either individually or as a group, the priest must make atonement for you by offering the appropriate sacrifices. The same applies to you and to the strangers and foreigners living among you.

"'Those who sin intentionally and defiantly, showing open contempt for the Lord, have condemned themselves and should be put to death.'"

Later the people found a man working on the Sabbath, so they brought him to Moses and Aaron, who asked the Lord what to do. The Lord said, "Because of his public defiance of what I have said, the man should be put to death." So the people took the man outside the camp and stoned him to death.

Then the Lord announced to Moses, "I want My people to be distinct in their dress. They should put a blue border and small blue tassels on the hem of their garments to remind them of who they are, that they belong to Me, and as a sign that they have committed themselves to keeping My commandments. I am the Lord who brought them out of slavery in Egypt—I am their God" (Num. 15).

Another Rebellion

Now Korah, a descendant of Levi, together with Dathan and Abiram, persuaded 250 other leaders to join them in challenging Moses. Why do you and Aaron assume such authority and think you're better than anyone else?" they demanded of Moses. "Everyone is just as good as you are."

Stunned, Moses said to Korah, "Let the Lord decide who the leader should be. Come back tomorrow with your censers to worship the Lord, and we'll see what He says. Don't forget how good the Lord has already been to the tribe of Levi by choosing you to work for Him at the sanctuary. And now you want to be priests and do what Aaron does and take over the leadership of Israel too?"

Then Moses sent for Dathan and Abiram so that he could talk to them as well, but they refused, saying, "Why does Moses act like a king? He brought us out of Egypt, but he still hasn't taken us into Canaan. We're not coming."

When Moses heard what they had said, he was deeply hurt and said to the Lord, "What is it with these men? I haven't done a thing to them or taken anything from them." Turning to Korah, he said, "Tomorrow we'll see what the Lord has to say."

The next day Korah and the people who supported him came to see how God would respond. Suddenly the glory of the Lord appeared above the sanctuary, and He said to Moses, "You need to step aside and let Me consume these rebellious people."

Moses and Aaron then fell to their knees and pleaded, "Lord, please don't punish all these people because of these men!"

"Tell the people to go back to their tents and to stay away from the tents of Korah, Dathan, and Abiram," the Lord replied.

After Moses told them, he added, "We'll see what the Lord says. If nothing happens, then the Lord did not choose me as your leader. But if something unusual takes place, such as the earth splitting open and all of them falling in, that will show they have rebelled against the Lord."

So the people quietly went back to their tents, and Korah, Dathan, and Abiram and their families stood defiantly in front of theirs.

No sooner had the people gone back to their tents than the earth split wide open, and all three men, along with their families and everything they had, slid into the opening, and the earth closed back up. When their supporters saw this, they cried out in fear and ran away as fast as they could. But instead of repenting, they defended the actions of Korah and his two friends, and fire came out from the presence of the Lord and more than 200 of their sympathizers perished.

The Lord said to Moses, "Tell Eleazar, Aaron's son, to collect the censers of these rebellious Levites who died and hammer them into a bronze sheet to cover the sacrificial altar. This will help the people to remember what happened today." So that's what Eleazar did.

The next day the people declared to Moses and Aaron, "You two are to blame for killing those people!"

Suddenly the glory of the Lord shone above the sanctuary, and God said to Moses, "Get out of the way so that I can consume these people."

Moses turned to Aaron and said, "Quick! Take your censer with its hot coals and incense and go among the people, because the plague has already begun!" Aaron ran, got his censer, and went among the people, and the plague stopped.

That day more than 14,000 people died, in addition to the followers of Korah. It ended the rebellion and settled the question of Moses' leadership. Then Aaron returned to the sanctuary, where all this time Moses had been praying (Num. 16).

Leadership

Then the Lord said to Moses, "Ask each of the tribal leaders to bring you a walking stick, and write each man's name on his, with Aaron's name on the one representing the tribe of Levi. Take those walking sticks and place them in front of the ark in the Most Holy Place. The man whose stick produces blossoms is the one I have chosen to serve as priest. This should stop any questions the people have about who is to be priest."

So that is what Moses did, and the next day he went into the Most Holy Place to get the walking sticks to see what had happened. Aaron's stick was the one that had buds, blossoms, and even ripe almonds on it! Moses gave all of the other men their walking sticks back, and their rods looked the same as they had the day before.

Then the Lord asked Moses to take Aaron's stick back into the Most Holy Place and leave it there as a witness against the rebellion and to stop any further questions about the priesthood that might come up.

When the people saw what had happened, they were afraid to go near the sanctuary for fear they might die (Num. 17).

Duties and Support of the Priests

The Lord said to Aaron, "I have chosen you and your sons to serve as priests, and I have given you the tribe of Levi as helpers. You are to minister at the sanctuary, and the Levites will do the additional work.

"I have given the tithe and part of the offerings to support you and your family and to provide for the Levites and their families."

To Moses the Lord said, "Tell the Levites to collect the tithe from the people. They will give a tenth of it to Aaron, the high priest, but the rest of it belongs to them. If the people give you tithe in produce, you may eat of it, but a tenth of it goes to Aaron. The tithe is holy, so don't mishandle it, or you'll die" (Num. 18).

Purification

"The laws of cleanliness and purification should be strictly followed," the Lord told both Moses and Aaron. "These laws apply to the priest who disposes of the bodies of animal sacrifices and to anyone who touches people who have died at home or in the field or who have been killed by the sword. They will be unclean for a day or a week, according to the regulations I gave you, and anything they touch or anyone who touches them must be purified as well. If they refuse to go through the purification ritual and come to the sanctuary unclean, they should be cut off from the community" (Num. 19).

Moses Makes a Big Mistake

While the people were camped at Kadesh, Moses' sister, Miriam, died and was buried there. Now Kadesh was a place with very little water, and the people complained to Moses and Aaron, saying, "If only we had died with Korah, Dathan, and Abiram and their followers, it would have been so much easier! Why are we way out here without enough water? Why did we ever leave Egypt?"

Moses and Aaron went into the sanctuary, fell on their knees, and prayed for help. The Lord said to Moses, "I want you and Aaron to lead the people to the rock that I will point out. Take your shepherd's rod along, and when you get there, ask the rock to give you water and it will."

So Moses and Aaron led the people to the rock and Moses said, "Listen, you rebels! You want water? We will give it to you!" Then he took his shepherd's rod, the same one he had used in Egypt, and in anger struck the rock twice, and water gushed out, enough for all the people and their animals.

"Because you didn't do what I said, but in anger struck the rock instead of speaking to it," the Lord said afterward, "you dishonored Me in front of the people. So you will not lead the people into Canaan, as I had planned." Although heartsick about what he had done, Moses still willingly submitted to his discipline.

Then Moses led the people from Kadesh to the border of Edom. From there he sent a message to the king of Edom asking permission to pass through his country on the way to Canaan. He promised its ruler that the Israelites would not take a thing from the land or from his people. But the king sent word, "I will not let you pass through my country. And if you don't turn around and go back, I'll come after you with the sword and force you back." So the Lord directed Moses to lead the people to go around Edom.

When Israel came to Mount Hor, the Lord instructed Moses, "Climb up to Mount Hor with Aaron and Eleazar. Aaron will not go into Canaan, either, because he also was upset with the people and dishonored Me in front of them. He will die on top of the mountain, and his son Eleazar will take his place."

Moses told Aaron what the Lord had said, and, together with Eleazar, they went up the mountain. At the top, Moses took Aaron's robe and put it on Eleazar. Aaron died there, and they buried him. Then Moses and Eleazar came down the mountain without Aaron, and when the people heard what had happened, they grieved and mourned for Aaron for a whole month (Num. 20).

Troubles Along the Way

Then the people broke camp and left Mount Hor and continued on their way. As they left, a king from one of the Canaanite cities attacked Israel from the rear and took some of the stragglers prisoner.

The people pleaded with the Lord to help them. He did, and they defeated the Canaanites, recovered the prisoners, and destroyed the city (Num. 21:1-3).

Poisonous Snakes

From Mount Hor the people made their way around the country of Edom. It wasn't long before they again complained to Moses, saying, "Why did you take us out of Egypt? Did you bring us out here to die? There's never enough food or water, and we're tired of eating manna."

So the Lord removed His protective hand, and poisonous snakes slithered out of the wilderness and into the camp. Some people were bitten and died, and others raced to Moses and said, "We have sinned by rebelling against you and the Lord! Pray and ask the Lord to take away these snakes!"

Moses prayed, and the Lord said, "Take a piece of metal, shape it into a snake, and put it high up on a pole. Whoever has been bitten and looks at the metal snake, believing that I can heal the serpent's bite, will be healed." And those who did so were healed (Num. 21:4-9).

Moving On

Then the people broke camp and followed the Lord wherever He led them, and when they needed water, the Lord provided it.

At the border of the little Amorite country, Moses sent word to Sihon, the king, asking permission to pass through his country. He promised that the people would stay on the main road and not touch a thing. The king refused and attacked the Israelites to drive them away, but Israel fought back, defeated the king, and took over the little country and made it their own.

Then Og, the king of Bashan, raided the Israelites. They defeated him, too, and seized his small kingdom as well (Num. 21:10-35).

The Donkey

From there the people traveled to the border of Moab, where they would cross the Jordan River into Canaan. Balak, its king, had heard how the Israelites had defeated the other two kings, and he was worried. So he decided to send messengers to Balaam, once a good man and a prophet of the Lord, asking him to curse Israel to weaken them.

Leaders from the local Midianites joined the delegation from Moab, and together they went to see Balaam, ready to pay him for his services. Balaam welcomed them, asked them to stay for the night, and told them that he would give them an answer in the morning.

During the night God spoke to Balaam in a dream and said, "Who are these men, and what do they want?"

"Balak, the king of Moab, sent them," the prophet answered. "He wants me to curse Israel."

"I don't want you to do that, because I have blessed Israel."

In the morning Balaam told the men that he couldn't go with them.

So they went back and told the king what happened, but the ruler didn't give up. He sent a higher-ranking delegation to Balaam, begging him to come and offering him even more money and greater honor.

"I can't go with you unless the Lord lets me," the prophet replied. "Stay overnight, and I'll give you an answer in the morning."

During the night the Lord spoke to Balaam in a dream and said, "If you insist, you may go, but I want you to bless My people, not curse them." In the morning Balaam told the men that he had permission to leave, that they should go on ahead, and that he would saddle his donkey and follow at his own pace.

To teach Balaam a lesson, God sent an angel with a drawn sword to block his way. Balaam didn't see the angel, but the donkey did and went into the field to get around the angel. That made Balaam angry, so he beat the animal. Then the angel went to a place on the road with low stone walls on either side. Again the donkey saw the angel and tried to get around him by squeezing against the wall, hurting Balaam's foot. This time Balaam really beat the donkey. Next the angel stood in an even narrower spot so that the donkey couldn't possibly pass by him. Unable to go on, the animal stopped and lay down. Balaam was beside himself and this time beat the donkey mercilessly.

The Lord gave the donkey a human voice, and it said to Balaam, "Why have you beaten me these three times?"

Without thinking about it, Balaam answered, "You've made a fool of me by making it appear that I don't even know how to ride a donkey. If I had a sword, I'd kill you."

"Haven't I been a faithful donkey? Have I ever done this before?"

"No."

Then the Lord opened Balaam's eyes, and he saw the angel standing on the road with a drawn sword. The prophet fell on his knees with his face to the ground and closed his eyes, afraid to look. The angel said, "Why did you beat your donkey these three times? If it had not seen me and stopped, you'd be dead."

"I didn't know you were there. I have sinned, so if you don't want me to go to Moab, I'm willing to turn around and go back home."

"No, go on. Follow the men, but you will say about Israel only what I will tell you."

When the king heard that Balaam was approaching, he went out to meet him and said, "What was the delay? Why didn't you come right away?"

"Well, I'm here now, but I can say only what the Lord allows me to say."

Then the king and his chief advisers took Balaam to one of the high places in Moab, where they offered sacrifices to Baal, and from there Balaam had a good look at Israel (Num. 22).

First Blessing

Balaam said to the king, "Let's build seven altars close together and offer seven bulls and seven rams on each. Then stay here with your officials while I go to be by myself and ask the Lord what to tell you."

He went a short distance and prayed to the Lord, asking Him what to do, and the Lord answered, "Go back to the king, and I will tell you what to say."

So Balaam went back, looked out at the camp of Israel, and said, "How can I curse the people whom the Lord has blessed? There are so many of them—it would be hard to count just one part of them. Let me be like them and die with them."

When the king heard that, he turned to Balaam and said, "What have you done? You have blessed Israel rather than cursing them!"

"I can say only what the Lord wants me to say," Balaam explained (Num. 23:1-12).

Second Blessing

"Come with me!" the king said. "Let's go to another place where you can see only part of Israel. That way you won't be so intimidated." They went to the top of Mount Pisgah and again built seven altars and offered the same number of sacrifices. Then Balaam said to the king, "You stay here while I go a short distance to see what the Lord will tell me this time." He prayed, and the Lord said to Balaam, "Go back, and I will let you know what to say."

When Balaam returned, the king asked, "Well, what has the Lord spoken?" Balaam looked out at Israel and said, "God does not lie or change His mind like a human being does. He does what He says He will do, and what He blesses, no one can change. He has forgiven Israel their sins, brought them out of Egypt, and is among them. Israel is like a lion, who does not lie down until it kills its prey and has its fill" (Num. 23:13-24).

Third Blessing

Then the king said, "If you can't curse Israel, at least don't bless them. Come with me. Let's go up to Mount Peor and look beyond the tents of Israel out toward the wilderness." So they went and built seven altars and offered sacrifices, as they had done before.

This time Balaam did not go back to the Lord for guidance. Instead, as he looked out toward the wilderness he noticed how orderly the tents of Israel were, each tribe in its place. "I am like a man whose eyes have been opened," he began, "one who hears words and has visions while wide awake. How beautiful are your tents, O Israel! God has brought you out of Egypt. He has given you the strength of a wild ox that is not afraid, who breaks the bones of the nations and then lies down like a satisfied lion" (Num. 23:25-24:9).

Israel's Future

When the king heard that, he was extremely angry. "I asked you to come and curse Israel, but you've blessed them three times!"

"I told your delegation that even if they gave me a house full of gold and silver," Balaam replied, "I could say only what the Lord allows me to say. Now let me tell you about Israel's future, and then I'll go back home.

"A star will come out of Jacob, and a king from Israel. Under His leadership they will take over Edom and defeat all their enemies. Who can possibly stop God when He does this?"

Then Balaam thanked the king and went back home, and the king returned to his palace (Num. 24:10-25).

Tricked Into Sin

At the suggestion of Balaam before he left, Balak invited the Israelites camped at the border of Moab to join them in a religious festival. Many of them, including the tribal leaders, accepted the king's invitation and crossed the border into Moab. They ate and drank with the Moabites and, at the height of the festival, joined them in worshipping Baal and in having sex with the Moabite women as part of their idol worship.

The Lord was angry with what He saw and said to Moses, "Will these people ever learn? When the tribal leaders and the other men who participated in this worship come back, tell the judges that they must issue an order for them to be executed for what they have done." And that's what Moses did.

Now one of the tribal leaders had brought a woman back with him, passing right by the sanctuary while the people were weeping and praying about what had happened. When Phinehas, Aaron's grandson, saw this, he followed the man to his tent and thrust his spear through both of them. Then the plague that the Lord had sent on Israel because of this immoral worship stopped, but not before 24,000 people had died.

The Lord said to Moses, "Because Phinehas did not allow such open defiance but upheld the honor of My name, I decided to stop the plague and extend to him and his family a covenant of peace. His descendants will always be a part of the priesthood of Israel."

The man who had brought the woman to his tent was Zimri, one of the leaders from the tribe of Simeon. The woman was Cozbi, the daughter of one of the leaders of the Midianites.

"Don't forget that the Midianites and the Moabites work together and that both are your enemies," God reminded Moses. "It was the Midianite women who participated in this national festival that were the most aggressive in seducing My people" (Num. 25).

Another Census

Then God instructed Moses and Eleazar, the son of Aaron, "Take a census of the men in Israel from 20 years old and up who are able to go to war."

So they did, beginning with the tribe of Reuben, and the final count for all of Israel was more than 600,000 men ready for war.

After the census, the Lord said to Moses, "I want you to divide the land of Canaan according to tribes by drawing lots. The larger tribes should have larger sections and the smaller tribes, smaller portions, except for the Levites, who are to live among all the people."

Moses and Eleazar had conducted the census on the east side of the Jordan River across from Jericho and found that there was not a man living from the first census that Moses and Aaron had done 40 years before in the wilderness of Sinai, except Caleb and Joshua (Num. 26).

Inheritance

Now some daughters from the tribe of Manasseh came to Moses and Eleazar and said, "Our father died in the wilderness and left no sons. How can we retain our family name without an inheritance?"

Moses asked the Lord what to do. The Lord answered, "If a man dies and has no sons, the inheritance goes to the daughters. But if there are no daughters, it passes to his brothers. Should there be no brothers, his uncles will receive it. And if there are no uncles, it will belong to the closest relative" (Num. 27:1-11).

Transfer of Leadership

Now the Lord said to Moses, "Go up the mountain, and from there you will be able to get a look at the land of Canaan. I cannot let you go in, because at Meribah you struck the rock with your staff in anger and told the people that you would bring water out of the rock. You took the honor to yourself, so you will go to your rest, just as your brother, Aaron, did."

"Lord, my life is in Your hands. But that means the people will need a new leader."

"I have chosen Joshua, who has an excellent spirit. Take him to Eleazar, the high priest, at the sanctuary. Call the people together and, in front of everyone, lay your hands on Joshua, transferring authority to him."

So Moses took Joshua to Eleazar and publicly passed the responsibilities of leadership to Joshua (Num. 27:12-23).

Rules for Sacrifices and Offerings

Then the Lord gave Moses the following instructions: "The people are to bring their offerings to Me at the times designated by the priests.

"And the priests are to offer one lamb in the morning and one in the evening. On Sabbath they should offer two lambs with flour, grain, and oil, in addition to the daily offerings.

"At the beginning of each month, they should add to the daily offerings two young bulls, one ram, and seven lambs with oil, grain, flour, and unfermented wine.

"And the Passover is like the Sabbath. No regular work should be done. The extra offerings on that day should be the same as at the beginning of each month.

"The Festival of Harvest is also a Sabbath. The extra offerings on that day should be the same as those on the Passover.

"The first day of the seventh month is the Festival of Trumpets. Like the Passover, no regular work should be done, and the extra offerings should be only one bull instead of two, but still one ram and seven lambs with flour and oil. However, the priests are to add a young goat as a sin offering.

"The tenth of that month is the Day of Atonement. The additional offerings are to be the same as those on the Festival of Trumpets, plus the regular sin offering.

"For one week, beginning on the fifteenth of the seventh month, is the Festival of Booths, reminding the people of their deliverance from Egypt. On the first day of that week you should offer 13 young bulls, two rams, 14 lambs, and flour and oil, and one young goat. Every day during that week the offerings should be the same, except for one bull fewer each day" (Num. 28:1-29:40).

Vows

Then Moses spoke to the people about vows and said, "If a man makes a vow to do something or give something to the Lord and confirms it with an oath, he must not break his word.

"If a woman still living with her parents makes a vow and confirms it with an oath, then tells her father and he agrees to it, it will stand. But if he does not approve, the Lord will release her from her vow.

"The same rule applies to a married woman and her husband. He may confirm the vow or release her from it, and the Lord will accept his decision. If he says nothing one way or the other when he first hears about it but later wants to release her from it, he's guilty of breaking the vow.

"If a widow or a divorced woman makes such a vow, it will stand" (Num. 30).

War

After these instructions, the Lord gave the Israelites permission to attack the Midianites, who were their worst enemies. So Moses took 1,000 men from each tribe and told them to get ready for battle, and asked Phinehas, the son of Eleazar, to be in charge of giving signals with the silver trumpet.

The Israelites went into battle and killed five Midianite kings and all their men, including Balaam, the apostate prophet. They took their women and children as captives, along with their flocks and herds.

When the Israelites returned, Moses and Eleazar went out to meet them. It upset Moses greatly when he saw that they had brought home the women who had earlier led the people into idolatry and the sexual worship of Baal. He ordered the officers to execute these women, along with the Moabite young men who would soon be ready for war, but to spare the young boys and girls.

Then he commanded the men to wash their clothes and purify themselves for one week before coming back into camp. The plunder of war was to be divided among the troops and the people. Also, he had the troops pay a tax on their plunder and give it to Eleazar, the priest, as an offering to the Lord. Moses and Eleazar accepted the gold from the men and brought it into the sanctuary (Num. 31).

Settling in the Land

The tribes of Reuben and Gad saw that the land east of the Jordan River offered good grazing for their flocks and herds. So they asked Moses to let them settle there and not have them cross the Jordan and reside in Canaan.

"Do you mean to stay here and not go with your brothers into Canaan?" Moses asked. "If you want to settle here, that's fine, but if you don't fight alongside them, that will discourage the other tribes. The Lord will not be happy and may let you die here and allow only the next generation into Canaan, as He did to your fathers when they first came out of Egypt."

"We'll make arrangements for someone to take care of our animals," they answered, "and then we'll go with our brothers and fight alongside them. After Canaan has been taken, we'll come back here." Moses agreed and told them to get ready for war, then added, "If you don't keep your promise, your sin will come back on you."

Half the tribe of Manasseh also saw that the land east of the Jordan would make good grazing land. So they decided to live there, too, and made the same arrangements with Moses as the tribes of Reuben and Gad had (Num. 32).

Review

Moses recorded everything that God had done for Israel from the time

126

they left Egypt until they were ready to cross the Jordan River and enter Canaan (Num. 33:1-49).

Canaan

Then the Lord spoke to Moses and said, "When you cross the Jordan and go into Canaan, you must ask the Canaanites to move out and settle elsewhere, and then you need to destroy their idols and places of worship. If you don't, the people and their places of worship will be like irritants in your eyes and thorns in your side. And if you become like them, I will have to force you out too" (Num. 33:50-56).

Boundaries

"The land of Canaan is to have borders to protect you and the rights of your neighbors. Your southern border will extend to the Red Sea by the border of Egypt, and your western border will go to the Mediterranean. Your northern border will be Mount Hor, and your eastern border will be east of the Sea of Galilee, then down the Jordan River to the Dead Sea.

"The tribes of Reuben, Gad, and half the tribe of Manasseh may settle east of the Jordan as they wanted to. Eleazar, Joshua, and one leader from each tribe are to decide how to divide the land" (Num. 34).

The Levites

Then God instructed Moses about the Levites, saying, "Give the Levites cities to live in among the 12 tribes, including some land for their animals. The larger tribes should provide the Levites more cities and land than the smaller tribes" (Num. 35:1-8).

Cities of Safety

The Lord continued, "Also designate certain cities as places of safety. If a person accidentally kills someone, they can go to one of these cities and feel safe from revenge until their case is heard. There should be six of these cities, three on each side of the Jordan River.

"If a person kills someone on purpose, they should be executed. If a person hits someone in anger and the victim dies but the person did not intend to kill them, that person can flee to one of these cities, and the people there should hear the case. If it is decided that it does not warrant the death penalty, that person should remain in that city until the death of the high priest.

"During the trial, there should be two or three witnesses. One witness is not enough. If the case is clearly murder, no ransom should be accepted to lessen the sentence or to set the accused person free" (Num. 35:9-34).

Marriage

Now the heads of families came to Moses and said, "The Lord told us that if we had no sons, the land should go to the daughters. But our question is What happens if our daughters marry someone from another tribe? Does our family property go with her? That would mean people from other tribes will own our land, and if the land changes hands for whatever reason, it will always go back to that tribe during the year of jubilee."

"Daughters who have inherited tribal land may marry whomever they want," Moses explained, "but must marry someone from their own tribe. This way each family will keep its own land, and so will each tribe."

Moses' Faithfulness

All that the Lord had said and the instructions He had given to Israel through Moses before they crossed the Jordan River into Canaan were faithfully carried out and recorded (Num. 36).

ten

Deuteronomy: Moses' Final Instructions

Moses spoke to the people while they were still east of the Jordan and reminded the new generation of what God had done for them and the importance of obeying the Lord.

"May the God of your fathers bless you and increase you a thousand-fold," he said to them. "Soon after we came out of Egypt, I told your fathers that I could not carry the leadership alone and judge all the cases that kept coming to me. They needed to choose wise and understanding leaders from among the tribes to serve as judges to help carry the caseload. Your fathers did this, and I told those judges to hear all cases, small and great, and not to be partial or afraid to do things right. The cases too hard for them, they should bring to me.

"When we left Sinai, we went to the border of Canaan where the Amorites live. God told us not to be afraid but to move ahead. We sent in 12 men to look over the land and bring us a report. They came back and discouraged us from going in, except for Caleb and Joshua. Your fathers listened to the 10 and refused to go in. So the Lord told them that, because of their lack of faith after what they had seen Him do in Egypt, they would have to go back into the wilderness. While they acknowledged their disobedience, they also decided to fight the Amorites without the Lord's help. They returned in defeat and wept. So we left the borders of Canaan and headed back into the wilderness.

"Forty years have passed. During that time God has been with us and blessed us. Now we are headed for Canaan a second time. The Lord is still with us, and we have already defeated King Sihon and King Og, two very powerful rulers this side of the Jordan.

"When we reached the Jordan River, the tribes of Reuben, Gad, and half the tribe of Manasseh decided not to go over but to settle there. The Lord agreed to this plan, but expected the rest of the tribes to settle in Canaan. As you know, I will not be allowed to go into Canaan because of what I did at Meribah, when I struck the rock with my staff in anger and took credit for giving you water.

"The Lord said to me, 'Go to the top of Mount Pisgah and look west, north, south, and east. Take a good look at the land of Canaan, but I can't let you go in because of what you did'" (Deut. 1:1-3:29).

Don't Forget

Moses continued, "Do what the Lord has asked you to do, and He will help you as you enter Canaan and settle there. Don't add or subtract from what He has told you, because His words will give you understanding and wisdom. What other nation has such laws and guidance from God as you have? Don't forget what you have seen and heard and been taught, and teach these things to your children and grandchildren, especially what you saw and heard at Sinai when you were children and the whole mountain was on fire. The Lord spoke the Ten Commandments to us out of the midst of the fire and then wrote them on tablets of stone.

"Stay away from idolatry, and don't make images of anything and bow down to them. The Canaanites worship gods that can't see or hear. If you will seek God with all your heart, you'll find that He's very close to you and will never leave you or forsake you. Soon I have to leave you, so please take care of yourselves and keep His commandments, and things will go well with you and your children."

After Moses had set aside the three cities of safety on the east side of the Jordan, he called the people together again and said, "Listen to me. God made a covenant with us at Sinai based on the Ten Commandments and said, 'I am the Lord who brought you out of Egypt, so don't worship other gods. Don't make idols and worship them. If you do, there will be consequences that I cannot overlook. But I will bless those who love Me and obey My commandments. Honor My name—don't misuse it. Keep the Sabbath and don't work on that day or have others work for you. Remember that you were slaves in Egypt and I set you free— that's another reason for you to observe the Sabbath besides remembering Me as your Creator.

"'Honor and respect your parents. Don't commit murder. Don't commit adultery. Don't steal. Don't lie or give a false witness. Don't be jealous of your neighbor and want what he has, whether it is his wife, his house, or anything else he has.'

"Oh, that you would always love the Lord with all your heart and soul and keep His commandments! Don't turn to the right or to the left, but do what the Lord wants you to do, and all will go well with you.

"Listen, Israel, the Lord your God is one! Love Him with all your heart and soul and mind. Teach these commandments to your children and grandchildren, and don't forget to keep them yourself.

"After you've settled in Canaan and you're comfortable and well fed, don't forget what the Lord has done for you and begin worshipping other gods, as the neighboring nations do. Stay with the Lord, and do what's right and good.

"When your children ask you the meaning of what you believe, tell them about Egypt and how the Lord set you free. Explain to them about Sinai and what you saw and heard, and how the Lord spoke to you and gave you these commandments" (Deut. 4:1-6:25).

A Chosen People

Then Moses cautioned the people, saying, "When you get to Canaan, don't let your sons and daughters marry Canaanites, because they will turn your children's hearts away from the Lord. Destroy their idols, altars, and shrines.

"You are a chosen people, holy to the Lord, God's special treasure. The Lord did not choose you as His because you were so numerous or so great. You were the least of people, but He selected you because He loves you. God is faithful and keeps His covenant promise from generation to generation with those who love Him and obey His commandments.

"The Lord will love you, bless you, and multiply you. He will take away your sickness and diseases and make you a great people.

"You do not need to fear bigger and more powerful nations, because the Lord is with you; He will deliver your enemies into your hand. So destroy their idols and don't covet their silver and gold, or you'll be headed for destruction, as they are.

"Every commandment the Lord gave us is important. Never forget how He brought you out of Egypt and guided you these 40 years and tested your faith to show you what was in your hearts.

"He allowed you to go hungry and then gave you manna to let you know that we are not to live by bread alone, but by every word that comes from the mouth of the Lord. Just as a father disciplines a son, so the Lord disciplined you.

"When the Lord brings you into Canaan, a rich and fertile land, don't forget Him and how He has blessed you. When you build beautiful houses and have all you need, don't tell yourself that it was your power and might that got you to where you are.

"The Lord is the one who gives you the power and strength to accomplish things and to get what you have. So don't forget the Lord, or you'll surely perish. What I'm telling you is true" (Deut. 7:1-8:20).

Reflections

Then Moses quickly reviewed the past 40 years of Israel and said, "You are now on the borders of Canaan and will soon cross the river Jordan and enter the land that the Lord promised to give you. Don't think that God will go with you because you're so righteous. You are actually a very stubborn people.

"Remember what happened at Sinai, how you provoked the Lord while I was up on the mountain? I was with the Lord for 40 days, and He gave me two tablets of stone with the Ten Commandments on them, which He had written with His own finger.

"You were down below worshipping the golden calf. The Lord was upset and wanted to destroy you and make from me a new nation. When I came down the mountain and saw what you were doing, I was so disgusted and angry that I threw the two tablets of stone down so hard that they broke into pieces. Then I destroyed the golden calf you had been worshipping and pleaded with the Lord that He not destroy you. I was worried not only about you, but about the Lord's reputation, fearing that the nations would think He was a weak god, powerless to bring you into Canaan, and that they might conclude that's why He destroyed you. The Lord heard my prayer, and as a result you are here today.

"Then the Lord asked me to make two new tablets of stone and bring them up the mountain, which I did. He wrote on them the Ten Commandments, as He had on the first tablets, and asked me to put them into the ark in the sanctuary. That's where they are today.

"What does the Lord require of you? He wants you to love Him with all your heart and soul, to walk in His ways, and to keep His commandments. Circumcise your hearts by cutting away the skin of sin and rebellion, and respect the Lord and serve Him. Give justice to the fatherless and widows. Love the stranger and foreigner who have come to live among you, not forgetting that you were once strangers and foreigners in Egypt yourselves.

"Hold on to the Lord, for He is your God; so let Him, and not other gods, be your praise. Don't forget what He has done for you, and love the Lord with all your heart and soul and obey His commandments. If you do this, you will become strong and add years to your life. The Lord will bless your land and give you rain in due season, and your fields, orchards, and vineyards will produce more than you need.

"Don't let yourselves be deceived or go astray and end up serving other gods. Take my advice to heart, and teach these things to your children and grandchildren. Write them down and remind each other to love the Lord, keep His commandments, and walk in His ways. Then the Lord will help you defeat your enemies, and the land of Canaan will be yours, from the Euphrates River to the Mediterranean Sea, from the mountains of Lebanon to the borders of Egypt.

"I'm giving you a choice, and what you decide will be a blessing or a curse to you. So when you cross the Jordan River heading into Canaan, go first to Mount Gerizim and Mount Ebal and repeat the blessings and curses across the valley that I will write out for you. Don't forget what I'm telling you" (Deut. 9:1–11:32).

Worship

"When you get to Canaan," Moses continued, "utterly destroy the pagan altars, the images of their gods, and their places of worship in the mountains. Worship the Lord, bringing sacrifices from your own flocks and herds, not theirs.

"Don't just do what you think is right, taking your offerings and sacrifices to whatever place you fancy, but bring them to the place that the Lord has chosen. You may worship the Lord in your own village and offer your sacrifices to Him there only if you live too far away to come.

"Don't forget the Levites who live among you, but support them and their families as long as they're there. Don't eat meat with blood still in it, as the Canaanites do, but follow the laws of health the Lord has given you" (Deut. 12).

False Prophets

"If some among you claim to be prophets and say that they have had dreams from the Lord, be careful. Even if they make predictions that actually happen, but then tell you that it's all right to worship other gods in addition to the God of Israel, don't believe them. They're false prophets. The Lord is letting this happen to test you to see if you love Him with all your heart and soul—to see if you are holding on to His commandments and worshipping Him alone. All false prophets should be put to death.

"If your parents, children, or one of your friends tells you it's all right to worship other gods also, don't do it, and don't defend them. They, too, should be put to death.

"If you hear that a group of people are trying to persuade a village to worship other gods in addition to the Lord, investigate it. If it's true, those people should be put to death, along with those who obeyed them. Worship the Lord only, and keep His laws and His commandments" (Deut. 13).

Additional Instructions

"Don't mourn for your dead loved ones the way the Canaanites do, who shave their heads and cut themselves," Moses continued. "You are God's children, a holy people, chosen by God as a special treasure above any other people on the face of the earth. Your hope is in Him!

"Follow the health principles and the diet the Lord has outlined for you. Eat meat from only animals that have split hooves and also chew the cud, only fish that have fins and scales, and only fowls and birds that are not scavengers. Most important, don't eat animals that died on their own.

"Bring your tithes to the Lord, whether it's a tenth of your harvests or of the increase of your livestock. If it's too far for you to bring all that to the sanctuary, exchange it for money. And don't forget the Levites, the foreigners, the widows, and the orphans—look after them.

"Also remember that every seventh year, all debts are to be canceled. The Lord will bless you for it. You can lend money to other nations, but don't borrow money from them, because it puts you under obligation to them, and you'll forget the needs of your own people. Take care of your poor. Don't just stand by and do nothing—help them. If you can aid someone who is poor by lending them money, do so, and don't worry about losing it if they can't pay you back on time. There will always be poor people among you, so help your brothers and sisters and don't ignore them.

"If a fellow Hebrew offers himself or herself to you as a servant to pay their debts, when the seventh year of release comes, you must let them go, whether they have worked it all off or not. And don't send them away empty-handed. Give them some of your animals, which will help them get back on their feet. Remember your time in Egypt and how you were treated, so be good to one another.

"All firstborn males from your flocks and herds belong to the Lord— they are not work animals. Don't forget that defective animals are not suitable for sacrifices. And let me remind you again that when you slaughter animals for food, be careful not to eat meat with blood still in it" (Deut. 14:1–15:23).

Festivals

Then Moses reviewed the guidelines for celebrating the Passover and the other festivals, and said, "Be sure to celebrate these festivals as families—sons and daughters, as well as servants, along with the larger family of God that includes the Levites, widows, and orphans. Everyone should give as they are able for the good of all.

"Remember that the Levites will have no inheritance of land. Their inheritance will come from a percentage of the animals and grain offerings brought to the sanctuary from the fields."

Concerning sacrifices, he said, "No defective animals should be sacrificed to the Lord, and nothing should be worshipped besides the God of heaven— not the sun, moon, stars, or any constellation. If anyone does so, and it is confirmed by two or three witnesses, the individual should be put to death."

Moses reminded the judges that they should not accept bribes or in any other way pervert justice.

Kings and Culture

"When you come into Canaan and want to have a king as other nations do," Moses continued, "the Lord will choose one from among you. No foreigner should rule over you, for he will lead you away from the Lord.

"Your king should not have multiple wives as other kings do, neither is he to accumulate huge amounts of silver and gold for himself. He should write for himself a copy of the laws the Lord gave us, including the rules for priests. Then he should read them often and be careful to do everything the law says, so that he won't become proud and turn away from the God of Israel, either to the right or to the left.

"Don't adopt the customs of the Canaanites, such as making your sons and daughters walk through fire, or practicing witchcraft, sorcery, or fortune-telling, or casting spells, or trying to speak with the dead. It's because of these things that the Lord has turned against the Canaanites. As for you, worship the Lord our God and walk blameless before Him."

A New Prophet

Then Moses focused on the future and said, "God will raise up a new Prophet from among you with this promise: 'I will put My words in His mouth, and He will say whatever I tell Him. Those who refuse to listen to Him will be held responsible. But if someone also claims to speak for other gods, they should be put to death. However, should anyone speak in My name, do not look for signs and miracles, but wait and see what they have to say and what predictions they make. If what they predict does not happen, or if it happens and they then lead you away from Me, they are false prophets and should be put to death'" (Deut. 16:1–18:22).

Justice

Moses also talked to the people about the six cities of safety, three among the tribes on the east side of the Jordan River and three among the tribes that would cross the Jordan and settle in Canaan.

"If a person kills someone accidentally, they need to get to one of these cities as fast as they can so that a relative of the dead person won't kill them out of revenge. The Lord does not want innocent blood to be shed.

"On the other hand, if someone hates another person and intentionally kills them and then runs to one of those cities for safety, the elders of that city should bring the person who killed someone back home and turn them over to the dead person's relatives. No one should pity that person, for the Lord wants all murdering in the land to stop.

"No one should be convicted of a crime based on the testimony of one witness. It must involve at least two or three witnesses. If there's a question about the truthfulness of a witness, the judges should carefully investigate the case, and if the witness falsely accused someone, they should receive the same penalty as the one accused would have. This will make people think twice before accusing someone of something that they did not personally witness. The rule of law is to be a life for a life, an eye for an eye, a tooth for a tooth, a hand for a hand, and a foot for a foot.

"Also, no one should move a person's property line, because the Lord gave that person that land for their family's future security" (Deut. 19).

War

"When you go out to battle and see an army larger than yours, don't be afraid, for the Lord will be with you, just as He was with you when He brought you out of Egypt.

"Before you face the enemy, one of the priests should remind you of this and say, 'Don't be afraid—the Lord will go with you and fight for you.' Then the officers in charge should announce, 'If there is a man here who just got married, built a new house, or planted a new vineyard, let him go back home or his thoughts will be elsewhere and his hesitancy to fight will affect the courage of the rest of his fellow soldiers.'

"When you come to a city, first make an offer of peace. If the people accept it, let them live and work for you. If they refuse and decide to resist, take the city and kill all the men of war, but be kind to the women and children and protect their animals, orchards, and vineyards. The Canaanite cities should be completely destroyed, or you will be tempted to worship their images and sin against the Lord" (Deut. 20).

"When you go to war and see a beautiful woman among the captives and you decide to marry her, bring her home to your house. Let her shave her head and mourn for the loss of her city and family for 30 days—then you can marry her. If she is not happy living in Israel and displeases you, you are not to mistreat her but set her free" (Deut. 21:10-14).

Domestic Concerns

"If you find someone's body in a field and it looks as if the person has been murdered, the elders of the nearest city will be responsible for settling the case and making atonement for the murder. This way they will put away the guilt of innocent blood from the land.

"If a man has taken two wives and loves one more than the other, and if the one he loves less has a son first, that son will have the rights of the firstborn, not the son of the wife he loves the most.

"If a man has a stubborn, rebellious son who drinks and won't listen to anyone, even after he's disciplined, the parents should bring him to the elders of the city, and if the elders find that this is true, he should be stoned to death.

"And if a person commits a sin worthy of death and is executed and the body is hung from a tree, it must be taken down and buried before nightfall.

"If you see an animal that has strayed and you recognize that it belongs to your neighbor, you should return it. If you don't know to whom the animal belongs, you should take it home and care for it until the rightful owner is found.

"When you see a nest in a tree or on the ground, you may take the eggs or the young ones, but don't take the mother.

"When you build a house with a flat roof, you must put a banister around the roof so that no one falls off and gets hurt.

"If a man marries a woman and then doesn't want her and spreads the rumor that she was not a virgin, her parents should go to the elders and give evidence to the contrary. If the evidence is confirmed, the elders should have the husband publicly whipped and order him to pay a fine. If she claimed she was a virgin and it has been proven otherwise, she should be stoned to death.

"If a man and another man's wife commit adultery, both should be stoned to death. The same holds true if a young woman is engaged and commits adultery with a man who knows she's engaged—both should be put to death. But if the man raped her, only he should be stoned to death. If a man seduces a young woman who is not engaged, he must be fined, and then he must marry her and never divorce her.

"A man should not sleep with his father's wife, even if she is not his mother. A woman should not dress like a man or a man like a woman. All these things are an abomination to the Lord" (Deut. 21:1-22:30).

Community Responsibility

Moses continued, "No one should be allowed into the sanctuary courtyard where the congregation worships who has been mutilated in his private parts. Nor should anyone born of an illegitimate relationship, for the sanctuary is holy.

"The Ammonites and Moabites are not allowed into the courtyard, even though they are descendants of Lot. They didn't give you water when you were thirsty, and they used Balaam to curse you and lead you into idolatry.

"The Edomites and Egyptians living among you who identify themselves with you may come into the courtyard to worship with the congregation. The Edomites are the descendants of Esau, Jacob's brother, and the Egyptians let Joseph bring his father and brothers into their land.

"Keep your communities clean. For your troops to relieve themselves, they should dig a hole outside the camp and then cover it up so there's no exposed waste. And if a man has an unexpected emission during the night, in the morning he ought to go outside the camp and wash himself and not come back until evening. The Lord is living among you, so keep yourselves and your places clean.

"If a slave runs away from their master and you find them, you are not to return them to their master, but take them home and treat them well. Then you are to give them the freedom to choose where they want to live.

"No Israelite woman or man should become a religious prostitute, even to make money for the Lord, nor should such money be accepted as an offering—it's an abomination.

"Don't charge your fellow Hebrews interest on money they borrow. If a non-Israelite borrows money from you, it's not wrong to charge him interest.

"When you promise to give or do something for the Lord, don't back out on what you vowed to do.

"When you're hungry and passing through your neighbor's vineyard or field, you can satisfy your hunger, but you are not to carry anything away.

"If a man divorces his wife and she remarries and the second husband also divorces her, the first one is not to take her back. Don't bring such wickedness into Israel.

"A man who just got married or started a business should not go out to war. He should stay home for a year.

"If someone kidnaps a person and then mistreats or sells the individual as a slave, they should be put to death.

"Don't oppress a hired servant. Pay them their wages at the end of each day, because they need to feed their family.

"Do not pervert justice. Fathers should not be put to death for the crimes of their children, nor should children be executed for the crimes of their father. Also make sure that strangers, the fatherless, and widows are treated with compassion. Never forget how you were treated in Egypt.

"When you harvest your fields, orchards, or vineyards, leave a little for the poor, the strangers, the fatherless, and the widows.

"If a dispute occurs between two people and they come to court and the judge orders the guilty one to be whipped, they should never get more than 40 lashes.

"When two brothers live near each other and share property and one of them dies, the widow should not marry a stranger or someone outside the family. The other brother should marry her, and his brother's property will go to her firstborn son. If the brother does not want to marry her, she should tell the elders of the city, and they should urge him to marry her. If he refuses, they should order the woman to take one of his sandals off his foot and spit in his face. Then he will always be known as the man who had his sandal pulled off.

"If two men get into a hand-to-hand fight, and the wife of one of them wants to save her husband and violently grabs the testicles of the other man and injures him so that he is not able to have children, she should have her hand cut off.

"Be honest in all your dealings, using the same weights and measures for everyone, no matter who they are. The Lord is not pleased when His people cheat.

"Don't forget what the Amalekites did to you when you came out of Egypt. They attacked, killing those who were weak and exhausted and who straggled behind. So when they attack you again, show no mercy" (Deut. 23:1-25:19).

A Special People

Moses reminded the tribes how the Lord had brought them out of Egypt and that they were a special people. "When you settle down," he said, "put some of the first produce of your fields in a basket, bring it to the Lord, and tell Him how grateful you are to be His people. Also lay aside an extra tenth of your produce and income every third year to provide for the poor, the fatherless, and the widows.

"You are special to the Lord, so keep His commandments. He will bless you above all others to be an honor and praise to His name."

Then Moses added, "When you cross the Jordan River, you are to set up two large stones and write on them the laws of God. Six tribes should stand on Mount Ebal and six on Mount Gerizim, and Joshua and the Levites will stand in the valley below and read each blessing and curse of disobedience. After each one that is read, the tribes shall respond with a hearty 'Amen.'

"God is displeased with anyone who treats their parents with contempt, who moves their neighbor's boundary line, who forces a blind person off the road, who perverts justice, who practices incest, who attacks their brother, or who takes a bribe.

"If you obey God's law, He will bless you in the city and in the country. He will bless your herds and flocks, your farms, and your work. As a result you will lend to other nations and need not borrow. You will be the head and not the tail.

"But if you don't live by God's commandments, there will be consequences. You will be a sickly people while your land will lose its productivity, it will lack rain, and locusts will destroy your crops. Foreigners will invade your land, take your wives and children, and slaughter your cattle. You will be scattered among the nations, find no resting place, and live in fear day and night" (Deut. 26:1–28:68).

The Covenant Renewed

Then the Lord asked Moses to lay out the terms of the covenant that He had made with the people at Sinai. So Moses called the people together and said to them, "You know what the Lord did for you when He brought you out of Egypt, and He has taken care of you all these years. Your clothes and sandals never wore out, and He fed you with the bread of heaven. He helped you defeat King Sihon and King Og, the two kings who attacked you, and then brought you safely to the borders of Canaan.

"So keep the covenant that the Lord made with you at Sinai and that He wants to renew with you today. This covenant is the same one He made with Abraham, Isaac, and Jacob. It's the same one He will make with your descendants for generations to come.

"The Lord does not want you to worship the gods of other nations. He does not want you to think that if you follow the dictates of your heart, you will have peace. Does a drunken person think the same as a sober one?

"Do you want to be a sickly people? Do you want your cities to be destroyed, as Sodom and Gomorrah were? If so, nations will say, 'Why did all this happen to these people who were so blessed? Well, it took place because they left the God of their fathers and worshiped other gods.'

"The covenant the Lord made with us and the things He revealed belong to us and our children forever. If you stray from the Lord but return and obey Him, He will have compassion on you and forgive you, and if you are scattered among the nations, He will bring you home again. Through His Spirit He will circumcise your heart and the hearts of your children to love the Lord your God with all your heart and soul and mind. He will bless all you do and rejoice over you, just as He did your ancestors.

"This covenant is not so hard that you can't keep it, and it's not so mysterious that you can't understand it. You don't have to go into the heavens or across the seas to find the Word of God—it is very close to you. You heard what the Lord said at Sinai, and you know that what He says, He means. You can never really forget God's word—it will always be in your heart and mind.

"So I'm giving you a choice. You can choose life or death, good or evil. If you don't want to listen to the Lord, you know what will happen. So choose life, obey the Lord, and cling to Him, for He is your life! Then you will live securely in the land that God promised to Abraham, Isaac, and Jacob" (Deut. 29:1–30:20).

Joshua, the New Leader

Next, Moses talked to the people about a new leader and said, "I'm 120 years old, and I can't come and go as I used to. Besides that, the Lord has told me that He can't let me accompany you into Canaan, because I took credit to myself for giving you water. But He will go with you and help you defeat your enemies, as He did with the two kings, Sihon and Og.

"So be strong and of good courage, and don't be afraid. The Lord is with you—He will not leave you or forsake you."

He turned to Joshua and, in front of all the people, said, "You will take my place and will have to guide them into Canaan. The Lord will not leave you or forsake you, but will go ahead of you; so don't be afraid, but lead with strength and courage."

Then Moses wrote out the rules of the covenant and gave them to the priests to place on the side of the ark. He told them to read the terms of the covenant to the people every seven years at the time of the Festival of Booths.

After that, the Lord said to Moses, "It is time for you to die. Call Joshua, and the two of you come to the sanctuary, where I will begin his leadership of Israel."

So Moses and Joshua went to the sanctuary, and the Lord appeared in the pillar of cloud and said to Moses, "You will rest with your forefathers. But the time will come when the people will worship other gods, and I will have to hide My face from them. So write a song to help them and their children remember Me and what I have done for them."

Then the Lord spoke to Joshua as Israel's new leader and said to him, "Be strong and of good courage to bring the people into the land of Canaan that I have promised them, and I will be with you."

Moses composed the song and asked the elders to assemble the people so that he could read it to them:

141

"Listen, O heavens! Hear me, O earth! Let my words be as the morning dew, as showers of rain on dry ground.

"Ascribe greatness to our God! He is the Rock. All His ways are just. He is the God of truth. He is righteous and upright in all that He does.

"Is He not our Father? Has He not brought us out of Egypt? Let us not forget what He has done for us. The Lord has protected us as the pupil of His own eye.

"If we turn against Him, He will remove His protection from us.

"How can one of us defeat a thousand, or two of us chase ten thousand, unless the Lord defeats our enemies? He is our Rock, the Rock of our salvation.

"He says, 'There are no other gods besides me. I am the one who gives life, and I am the one who takes it away. No one can take you out of My hand.'

"Let us rejoice! He will provide an atonement for His people!"

When Moses finished, he said, "Take this song to heart and remember what I have told you. These words are life to you, and they will help you live long and prosperous in the land where you are going" (Deut. 31:1-32:47).

Moses' Farewell

Then the Lord said to Moses, "Go to the top of Mount Nebo and get a good look at the land of Canaan before you die. I can't let you go in because of what you did when you took credit to yourself for getting water out of the rock for the people."

So Moses said goodbye to the people and blessed them, saying, "The Lord came down on Mount Sinai with thousands of angels and spoke to you. Not only did He give you His law, He loves you and holds you tightly in His hand.

"May Reuben, Judah, and Simeon be blessed—also Levi and Benjamin. May Ephraim and Manasseh (the two sons of Joseph) be precious in the Lord's sight. And may Zebulun, Issachar, Gad, Dan, Naphtali, and Asher always be strong for the Lord.

"Israel, how blessed you are! The eternal God is your refuge, and underneath are His everlasting arms. Who is like you, a people saved by the Lord?" (Deut. 32:48-33:29).

Moses Dies

Then Moses went to the top of Mount Nebo, the summit of Pisgah, and the Lord showed him the whole land of Canaan to the north, south, east, and west. God said, "I have given you the privilege of viewing the land I promised to Abraham, Isaac, and Jacob and their descendants. I have given you power to see it, but you can't go in."

So Moses died, and the Lord buried him on the mountain in the land of Moab, but no one knows where his grave is. He was 120 years old when he died, yet he still had good eyesight and strength. Israel wept for Moses and mourned for him for a whole month.

Joshua was now the new leader, and the people listened to him as the Lord had told them to do. But there was no one like Moses, who had talked with God face to face and who performed those awesome miracles in front of Pharaoh in Egypt and afterward in the sight of Israel (Deut. 34).

Other books by Jack Blanco that you may enjoy . . .

Savior
Four Gospels. One Story.

Take a fresh look at Jesus Christ, His ministry, and His teachings. This is the story of Jesus, the Messiah, God's beloved Son. With this simple introduction the story unfolds. But not as you've ever read it before. Combining these accounts chronologically and using contemporary language, Jack Blanco weaves Matthew, Mark, Luke and John together to form the beautiful timeless, captivating story on the life of Jesus, our Savior. 978-0-8127-0469-3

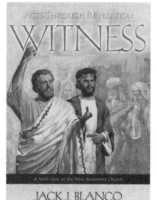

Witness
Acts Through Revelation

No matter what happened—threats, beatings, stoning, exile, or imprisonment—the leaders of the infant Christian church were determined to take the good news of Jesus' life, death, and resurrection to the entire world. That was their mission, their sole purpose in life. Written in modern language this is the message of God's love for humanity and the astonishing power of that love to change lives. 978-0-8127-0491-4

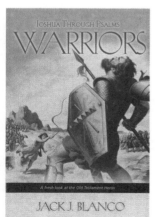

Warriors
Joshua Through Psalms

Jack Blanco, the author of the popular *The Clear Word* paraphrase, presents a harmony of Joshua, Ruth, 1 and 2 Samuel, 1 Chronicles and Psalms. The dramatic stories of prophets and kings are told in chronological order without the interruption of chapter or verses. It is a new and engaging way to read the Old Testament stories and to see God's hand working in the their lives. 978-0-8127-0511-9

Availability subject to change